ANDREW MURRAY

living the new LiFE

THE NEW LIFE

CONTENTS

TRANSLATOR'S NOTE

A glance at the pages of this work will show that it is more elementary than the other writings of its honored author. The reason is that it is designed especially for young disciples who have recently chosen the better part, and consequently need nothing so much as just to sit at the feet of Jesus and hear His Word. Every minister of a congregation in which young people have been brought to the Lord will remember the keen feeling of anxiety that swept over his heart as he contemplated their entrance into the duties and responsibilities of a public Christian confession. The supreme question at such a time is—how will these young converts be built up in the knowledge of the truth? How will they be best taught the real nature of the new life they have received, the dangers which are found there and the directions in which its energy may safely go forth?

The desire to give a fitting answer to these questions has given rise to many excellent manuals. In connection with every time of revival, especially, new books for this circle of readers always make their appearance. As Mr. Murray indicates in the Preface, it was in the midst of such a happy period that the following chapters were written. The volume came under my notice while I was recently traveling in Holland. A brief inspection showed me that it was one of the most simple, comprehensive, and helpful of its kind. It is now translated into English from the latest Dutch edition so that the many thousands who have profited from Mr. Murray's other admirable works may have a suitable book to give or recommend to those who are setting their faces toward an earnest and fruitful Christian life.

I cannot doubt that it will be very helpful to this end. Especially, if the directions the author himself has given are faithfully adhered to. It will be noticed that the chapters are relatively short, but every one of them has a considerable number of Biblical references. Let no reader be content to read what is written here without looking up and examining the texts marked. This practice, if persistently carried out, cannot fail to yield a great reward. There are just as many chapters in the book as Sundays in the year. What an additional blessing it would bring, if the members of a family who have had access to the book during the week were to hear a chapter read aloud every Sunday evening, and were each encouraged to quote the texts that may have struck them the most.

I have only to add that the volume is now translated and issued with Mr. Murray's cordial permission. It has been to me a very pleasant task to put it into an English translation for my younger brothers and sisters throughout the country. Of course, my responsibility does not go beyond this point. Should the book prove useful in guiding the feet of those who have come to the Lord yet further into the way of peace and holiness, it will be, both for author and translator, the answer to many fervent prayers.

J.P. Lilley

PREFACE

In speaking with young converts, I have very frequently longed for a suitable book in which the most important truths concerning the *new life* were presented briefly and simply. I could not find anything that entirely corresponded to what I desired. During the services in which I have been permitted to take part, I felt this need even more keenly. There I spoke with so many who professed to have found the Lord yet were still very weak in knowledge and faith. In the course of my journey, I have felt myself pressed to take my pen in hand.

Under a vivid impression of the infirmities and the distorted thoughts concerning the *new life*, with which almost all young Christians have to wrestle, I wished to offer them words of instruction and encouragement. I wanted to let them see what a glorious life of power and joy is prepared for them in their Lord Jesus, and how simple the way is to enjoy all this blessing.

I have confined myself in these reflections to some of the most important topics. The first is *the Word of God* as the glorious and sure guide, even for the simplest souls who will surrender themselves to it. Then, as the chief element in the Word, there is *the Son, the gift of the Father*, to do all for us. Then follows what the Scriptures teach concerning *sin*— as the only thing that we have to bring to Jesus, as that which we must give to Him, and from which He will set us free. Further, there is *faith*, the great word in which our inability to bring or to do anything is expressed, and that teaches us that all our salvation must be received every day of our lives as a gift from above. The young Christian must also make acquaintance with the *Holy Spirit* as the Person through whom the Word and Jesus—with all His work and faith in Him—can become power and truth. Then there is the *holy life* of obedience and fruitfulness, in which the Spirit teaches us to walk.

It is to these six leading thoughts of the *new life* that I have confined myself. In ceaseless prayer, I have asked that God use what I have written to make His young children understand what a glorious and mighty life they have received from their Father. It was often very unwillingly that I took leave of the young converts who had to go back to lonely places, where they could have little counsel or help, and seldom mingle in the preaching of the Word. It is my sure and confident expectation that what the Lord has given me to write will prove a blessing to many of these young confessors.

While writing this book, I have had a second wish abiding with me. I have wondered what I could possibly do to insure that my book would not draw attention away from the Word of God, but rather, help to make the Word more precious. I resolved to furnish the work with footnotes, so that, on every point that was referred to, the reader might be stirred up still to listen to *the Word itself*, to *God Himself*.

I am hopeful that this arrangement will yield a double benefit. Many a one does not know, and has nobody to teach him, how to examine the Scriptures properly. This book may help him in his loneliness. If he will only meditate on one point or another and then look up the texts that are quoted, he will get into the habit of consulting God's Word itself on whatever topic he wishes to understand. But, this book may just as readily be of service in prayer meetings or social gatherings for the study of the Word. Let each person read the chosen chapter at home and review the scripture verses that seem to be the most important to him. Let the leader of the meeting read the chapter aloud once. He should then invite each person who desires to, to share the verse or point which has meant the most to him.

We have found in my congregation that the benefit of such meetings for bringing and reading aloud verses on a point previously announced is very great. This practice leads to the searching of God's Word as even preaching does not. It stirs up the members of the congregation, especially the young people, to independent dealing with the Word. It leads to a more living fellowship among the members of Christ's body and also helps their upbuilding in love. It prepares the way for a social recognition of the Word as the living communication of the thoughts of God which, with divine power, will work in us what is pleasing to God.

I am persuaded that there are many believing men and women who ask what they can accomplish for the Lord—who along this path could become the channel of great blessing. Let them once a week bring together some of their neighbors and friends to read aloud the texts for which they have been previously searching. The Lord will certainly give His blessing there.

With respect to the use of this book in private, I would like to request one more thing. I hope that no one will think it strange. Let every portion be read over at least three times. The great poison of our conversation with divine things is superficiality. When we read anything and understand it somewhat, we think that this is enough. No, we must give it *time* so that it may make an impression and exercise its influence on us.

Read every portion *the first time* with consideration, to understand the good that is in it, and then see if you receive benefit from the thoughts that are expressed there.

Read it *the second time* to see if it is really in accordance with God's Word. Take some, if not all, of the texts that are cited on each point and ponder them in order to come under the full force of what God has said on the point. Let your God, through His Word, teach you what you must think and believe concerning Him and His will.

Read it *the third time* to find out the corresponding place, not in the Bible, but in your own life, in order to know if your life has been in harmony with the *new life*, and to direct your life in the future entirely according to God's Word. I am fully persuaded that the time and effort spent on such personal contact with the Word of God under the teaching of this or some other book that helps you in dealing with it, will be rewarded tenfold.

I conclude with a cordial, brotherly greeting to all with whom I have been permitted to mingle during the past year, in speaking about the precious Savior and His glorious salvation. Greetings also to all in other congregations, who in this last season have learned to know the beloved Lord Jesus as their Redeemer. With a heart full of peace and love, I think of all of you, and I pray that the Lord may confirm His work in you. I have not become weary of crying out to you: the blessedness and the power of the *new life* that is in you are greater than you know—are wonderfully great. Only, learn to know and trust completely in Jesus, *the gift of God*, and the Scriptures, *the Word of God*. Only give Him time to hold communion with you and to work in you, and your heart will overflow with the blessedness of God.

Now to Him who is able to do exceedingly more than we can ask or think, to Him be glory in the Church to all eternity.

Andrew Murray

Chapter 1
The New Life

"For God so loved the world, that He gave His only begotton Son, that whosoever believeth in Him should not perish, but have eternal life" John 3:16.

"For ye are dead, and your life is hid with Christ in God. Christ is our life" Colossians 3:3,4.

"We declare unto you the life, eternal life, which was with the Father and was manifested unto us. God hath given us eternal life; and this life is in His Son. He that hath the Son hath life" 1 John 1:2; 5:11,12.

A glorious blessing is given to all who believe in the Lord Jesus. Along with a change in his disposition and manner of living, he also receives an entirely new life from God. He is born anew. Born of God. He has passed from death into life.[1]

This new life is nothing less than eternal life.[2] This does not mean, as many suppose, that our life will no longer die, enduring into eternity. No, eternal life is nothing else than the very life of God. It is the life that He has had in Himself from eternity and that has been visibly revealed in Christ. This life is now the inheritance of every child of God.[3]

---

[1] John 1:12,13; 3:5,7; 5:24; 1 John 3:14; 5:1

[2] John 3:15,16,36; 6:40,51; 11:25,26; Rom. 6:11,23; 8:2; 1 John 5:12,13

[3] 1 John 1:3; 3:1; 5:11

This life is a life of inconceivable power. Whenever God gives life to a young plant or animal, that life has within itself the power to grow. The plant or animal as of itself becomes large. Life is power. In a new life—in your heart—there is the power of eternity.[4] More certain than the healthful growth of any tree or animal is the growth and increase of the child of God who surrenders himself to the working of the new life.

Two things hinder this power and the reception of the new spiritual life. The one is ignorance of its nature—its laws and workings. Man, even the Christian, cannot conceive of the new life which comes from God. It surpasses all of his thoughts. His own distorted thoughts of the way to serve and to please God—namely, by what he does and is—are deeply rooted in him. Although he believes that he understands and receives God's Word, he still thinks humanly and carnally on divine things.[5] God must give salvation and life. He must also give the Spirit to make us understand what He gives. He must point out the way to the land of Canaan. We must also, like the blind, be led by Him everyday.

The young Christian must try to cherish a deep conviction of his ignorance concerning the new life, and of his inability to form correct thoughts about it. This will bring him to the meekness and to the childlike spirit of humility, to which the Lord will make His secret known.[6]

---

[4]John 10:10,28; Heb. 7:16,28; 11:25,26; 2 Cor. 12:9; 13:4; Col. 3:3,4; Phil. 4:13

[5]Josh. 3:4; Isa. 4:5,6; Matt. 16:23

[6]Ps. 25:5,8,9; 143:8; Isa. 42:16; 64:4; Matt. 11:25; 1 Cor. 1:18,19; 2:7,10,12; Heb. 11:8

There is a second hindrance in the way of faith. In the life of every plant and every animal and every child of God, there lies sufficient power by which it can become big. In the new life, God has made the most glorious provision of a sufficient power. With this power His child can grow and become all that he must be. Christ Himself is his life and his power of life.[7] Yet, because this mighty life is not visible or cannot be felt, the young Christian often becomes doubtful. He then fails to believe that he will grow with divine power and certainty. He does not understand that the believing life is a life of faith. He must depend on the life that is in Christ for him, although he neither sees, feels, nor experiences anything.[8]

Let everyone then that has received this new life cultivate these great convictions. It is eternal life that works in me. It works with divine power. I can and will become what God will have me be. Christ Himself is my life. I have to receive Him everyday as my life, given to me by God, and He will be my life in full power.

Father, You have given me Your Son so that I may have life in Him. I thank You for the glorious new life that is now in me. I pray that You will teach me to properly know this new life. I will acknowledge my ignorance and the distorted thoughts which are in me concerning Your service. I will believe in the heavenly power of the new life that is in me. I will believe that my Lord Jesus, who Himself is my life, will, by His Spirit, teach me to know how I can walk in that life. Amen.

---

[7]Ps. 18:2; 27:1; 36:8,9; John 14:19; Gal. 2:20; Col. 3:3,4
[8]Hab. 2:4; Matt. 6:27; Rom. 1:17; Gal. 3:11; Heb. 10:38

Notes

Try to understand and plant the following lessons in your heart:

1. It is eternal life, the very life of God, that you have now received through faith.

2. This new life is in Christ, and the Holy Spirit is in you to convey to you all that is in Christ. Christ lives in you through the Holy Spirit.

3. This life is a life of wonderful power. However weak you may feel, you must believe in the divine power of the life that is in you.

4. This life needs time to grow in you and to take possession of you. Give it time, it will surely increase.

5. Do not forget that all the laws and rules of this new life are in conflict with all human thoughts of the way to please God. Be very much in dread of your own thoughts. Let Christ, who is your life and also your wisdom, teach you all things.

Chapter 2

The Milk Of The Word

"As newborn babes, desire the sincere milk of the word, that ye may grow thereby unto salvation" 1 Peter 2:2.

Beloved young Christians, hear what your Father has to say in this word. You have just recently given yourselves to the Lord and have believed that He has received you. You have received the new life from God. You are now as newborn infants. He will teach you in this word what is necessary so that you may grow strong.

The first point is: *you must know that you are God's children.* Hear how distinctly Peter says this to those just converted—"You have been born again," "you are newborn infants," "you are now converted," "you are now the people of God."[1] A Christian, however young and weak, must know that he is God's child. Only then can he have the courage to believe that he will make progress and the boldness to use the food provided in the Word. All Scripture teaches us that we must know and can know that we are children of God.[2] The assurance of faith is indispensable for a healthy, powerful growth in the Lord.[3]

---

[1] 1 Pet. 1:23; 2:2,10,25
[2] Rom. 8:16; 1 Cor. 3:1,16; Gal. 4:6,7; 1 John 3:2,14,24; 4:13; 5:10,13
[3] Eph. 5:8; Col. 2:6; 1 Pet. 1:14,18,19

The second point which this word teaches you is: *you are still very weak*, weak as newborn children. The joy and love which a new convert sometimes experiences do indeed make him think that he is very strong. He runs the risk of exalting himself and of trusting in what he experiences. He should nevertheless learn much about how he should become strong in his Lord Jesus. Endeavor to deeply feel that you are still young and weak.[4] Out of this sense of weakness comes the humility which has nothing in itself.[5] It therefore expects all from its Lord.[6]

The third lesson is: *the young Christian must not remain weak*. He must make progress and become strong. He must grow and increase in grace. God lays it upon us as a command. Concerning this point, His Word gives us the most glorious promises. It lies in the nature of the thing—a child of God must and can make progress. The new life is a life that is healthy and strong. When a disciple surrenders himself to it, the growth certainly follows.[7]

The fourth and principal lesson, the lesson which young disciples of Christ have the most need of, is: *it is through the milk of the Word that God's newborn infants can grow*. The new life from the Spirit of God can be sustained only by the Word of God. Your life, my young brothers and sisters, will largely depend on whether you learn to deal wisely and well with God's Word, whether you learn to use the Word

---

[4]1 Cor. 3:1,13; Heb. 5:13,14

[5]Matt. 5:3; Rom. 12:3,10; Eph. 4:2; Phil. 2:3,4; Col. 3:12 4:14; 1 Thess. 4:1; 2 Pet. 3:18

[6]Matt. 8:8,15,27,28

[7]Judg. 5:31; Ps. 84:7; 92:13,14; Prov. 4:18; Isa. 40:31; Eph.

from the beginning as your milk.[8]

See what a charming parable the Lord has given us here in the mother's milk. Out of her own life does the mother give food and life to her child. The feeding of the child is the work of the tenderest love. The child is pressed to the breast and is held in the closest fellowship with the mother. The milk is just what the weak child requires, food—gentle and yet strong.

Even so, the very life and power of God is found in His Word.[9] Through the Word, His tender love will receive us into the gentlest and most intimate fellowship with Himself.[10] From the Word, His love will give us what is needed for our weakness. Let no one suppose that the Word is too high or too hard for him. For the disciple who receives the Word and trustfully relies on Jesus to teach him by the Spirit, the Word of God will prove to be as gentle, sweet milk for newborn infants.[11]

Dear young Christians, would you continue standing, would you become strong, would you always live for the Lord? Then hear this day the voice of your Father—"As newborn babes, desire the sincere milk of the Word." Receive this Word into your heart and hold it firmly as the voice of your Father. Your spiritual life will depend on your use of the Word of God. Let the Word of God be precious to you above everything.[12]

---

[8]Ps. 19:8,11; 119:97,100; Isa. 55:2,3; 1 Cor. 12:11

[9]John 6:63; 1 Thess. 2:13; Heb. 4:12

[10]John 10:4

[11]Ps. 119:18; John 14:26; Eph. 1:17,18

[12]Ps. 119:14,47,48,111,127

Above all, do not forget, the Word is the milk. The sucking or drinking on the part of the little child is the inner, living, blessed fellowship with the mother's love. Through the Holy Spirit, your use of the milk of the Word can become warm, living fellowship with the living love of your God. Long very eagerly for the milk. Do not consider the Word something hard and troublesome to understand—in that way you lose all delight in it. Receive it with trust in the love of the living God. With a tender motherly love, the Spirit of God will teach and help you in your weakness. Always believe that the Spirit will make the Word in you life and joy—a blessed fellowship with your God.

Precious Savior, You have taught me to believe Your Word, and You have made me a child of God by that faith. Through that Word, as the milk of the newborn babes, You will also feed me. Lord, for this milk I will be very eager. I will long after it everyday. Teach me, through the Holy Spirit and the Word, to walk and converse everyday in living fellowship with the love of the Father. Teach me to always believe that the Spirit has been given to me with the Word. Amen.

Notes

1. What texts do you consider the best for proving that the Scriptures teach us that we must know we are children of God?
2. What are the three points in which the sucking child is to us an example of the young child in Christ in his dealing with the Word?

3. What must the young Christian do when he has little blessing in the reading of God's Word? He must set himself down through faith in fellowship with Jesus Himself and believe that Jesus will teach him through the Spirit, and so trustfully continue in the reading.

4. One verse chosen to meet our needs, read ten times and then laid up in the heart, is better than ten verses read once. Only as much of the Word as I actually receive and inwardly appropriate for myself is food for my soul.

5. Choose for yourselves what you consider one of the most glorious promises about making progress and becoming strong, and learn it by heart. Repeat it continually as the language of your positive expectation.

6. Have you learned to understand well what the great means for growth in grace is?

Chapter 3

God's Word In Our Heart

"Therefore shall ye lay up these My words in your heart and in your soul" Deuteronomy 11:18.

"Son of man, all My words that I shall speak unto thee receive in thine heart" Ezekiel 3:10.

"Thy word have I hid in mine heart, that I might not sin against Thee" Psalm 119:11.

"As newborn babes, desire the sincere milk of the word, that ye may grow thereby" (1 Peter 2:2). Every young Christian is taught that he must receive the Word of God as milk—as the living participation of the life and vine of God—if he is to grow. On this account it is of great importance to know how we must deal with the Word. The Lord says that we must receive it and lay it up in our heart.[1] The Word must possess and fill the heart. What does that mean?

The heart is the temple of God. In the temple there was an outer court and an inner sanctuary. So it is in the heart. The gate of the court is understanding. What I do not understand cannot enter into the heart. The Word enters into the court through the outer gate of understanding.[2] There it is kept by memory and reflection.[3] Still it is not properly in the

---

[1]Deut. 30:14; Ps. 1:2; 119:34,36; Isa. 51:7; John 5:38; 8:31; 15:7; Rom. 10:8,9; Col. 3:16
[2]Ps. 119:34; Matt. 13:19; Acts 8:30
[3]Ps. 119:15,16

heart. From the court there is an entrance into the innermost sanctuary. The entrance of the door is *faith*. What I believe, that will I receive into my heart.[4] Here it becomes secure in love and in the surrender of the will. Where this takes place, there the heart becomes the sanctuary of God. His law is there, as in the ark, and the soul cries out, "Thy law is within my heart."[5]

Young Christian, God has asked for your heart, your love, your whole self. You have given yourself to Him. He has received you and would have you and your heart entirely for Himself. He will make your heart full of His Word. What lies in the heart is dear because it is filled with joyful thoughts. God would have the Word in the heart. The Lord and His might are where His Word is. He considers Himself bound to fulfill His Word. When you have the Word, you have God Himself at work in you.[6] He wills that you would receive and lay up His words in your heart. Then He will greatly bless you.[7]

How I wish that I could bring all young Christians to simply receive that Word of their Father, "Lay up these My words in your heart." I wish they would give their whole heart to become full of God's Word. Resolve then to do this. Take pains to understand what you read. When you understand it, always take one or another word to remember and consider. Learn the words of God by heart. Repeat them to

---

[4] John 5:38; Acts 8:37; Rom. 10:10,17
[5] Ex. 25:16; Ps. 37:31; 40:8; Col. 3:16
[6] Gen. 21:1; Josh. 23:14
[7] Deut. 11:10; 28:1,2; Ps. 1:2,3; 119:14,45,98,165; John 17:6,8,17

yourself in the course of the day. The Word is seed and the seed must have time, must be kept in the ground. Likewise, the Word must be carried in the heart. Give the best powers of your heart, your love, your desire, the willing and joyful activity of your will, to God's Word.

"Blessed is the man whose delight is in the law of the Lord; and in His law doth he meditate day and night" (Psalm 1:1,2). Let the heart be a temple—not for the world and its thoughts—but for God and His thoughts.[8] If you faithfully open your heart to God's voice, hear His Word and carry it with you, you will discover how faithfully God will open His heart to you and hear your prayer.

Dear Christian, read once again the words at the beginning of this section. Receive them as God's Word to you—the Word of the Father who has received you as a child, of Jesus who has made you God's child. God asks of you, as His child, that you give your heart to become filled with His Word. Will you do this? What do you say? In this manner of power, the Lord Jesus will complete His holy work in you.[9] Let your answer be distinct and continuous, "Thy word have I hid in mine heart." "How love I Thy law! it is my meditation all the day" (Psalm 119:97). Even if it appears difficult for you to understand the Word, continue to read it. The Father has promised to make it a blessing in your heart. But you must take it into your heart first. Believe that God will then, by the Holy Spirit, make the Word living and powerful in you.

---

[8] Ps. 119:69; John 15:3,7; 17:6,8,17
[9] John 14:21,23; 1 John 2:14,24; Rev. 3:8,10

*My Father who has said to me, "My son, give Me
your heart," I will give You my heart. Now that You
charge me to lay up and keep Your Word in that
heart, I answer, "I keep Your commands with my
whole heart." Father, teach me to receive Your
Word in my heart everyday so that it can exercise its
blessed influence there. Strengthen me in the deep
conviction that even though I do not yet fully understand its meaning and power, I can still depend on
You to make the Word living and powerful in me.
Amen.*

Notes

1. What is the difference between the reading of
the Word to increase knowledge and the receiving of
it in faith?

2. The Word is as a seed. Seed requires time before
it springs up. During this time it must be kept silently
and constantly in the earth. I must not only read
God's Word, but ponder it and reflect on it. Then it
will work in me. The Word must be with me the
whole day, must abide in me, must live in me.

3. What are the reasons that the Word of God
sometimes has so little power in those who read it
and really long for blessing? One of the principal
reasons is surely that they do not give the Word time
to grow. They do not keep it and reflect on it in the
believing assurance that the Word itself will have its
working.

4. What is the first characteristic of His disciples
that Jesus mentions in the high-priestly prayer (John
17)?

5. What are the blessings of a heart filled with the
Word of God?

Chapter 4
Faith

"Blessed is she that believed; for there shall be a performance of the things which were told her from the Lord" Luke 1:45.

"I believe God, that it shall be even as it was told me" Acts 27:25.

"Abraham was strong in faith, being fully persuaded that what He had promised, He was able also to perform" Romans 4:20,21.

God has asked you to take and lay up His Word in your heart. The Word is taken and received into the innermost depths of your heart through the avenue of faith. Let the young Christian take pains to better understand what faith is. He will then gain an insight into the reasons why such great things are connected to faith. He will have a perfect belief in the idea that full salvation is dependent upon faith.[1]

Let me now ask my reader to read over the three texts which stand above. Find out what the principal thought is that they teach about faith. Please, do not read beyond them. First read these words of God and ask yourself what they teach you about faith.

They help us to see that faith always attaches itself to what God has said or promised. When an honorable man says anything, he also does it. So it is with God. Before He does anything, He reveals it through His Word. When the Christian becomes possessed

[1] 2 Chron. 20:20; Mark 9:23; Heb. 11:33,35; 1 John 5:4,5

26

with this conviction—established in it—God always does what He has said. With God, speaking and doing always go together. The deed always follows the Word. "Hath He said, and shall He not do it?" (Numbers 23:19).[2] When I have a Word of God in which He promises to do something, I can always be sure that He will do it. I simply have to believe the Word and wait upon God. God will fulfill His Word to me. Before I feel or experience anything, I hold onto that promise. I know by faith that God will make it good to me.[3]

What then is faith? *Nothing other than the certainty that what God says is true*. When God says that something exists, then faith rejoices although it sees nothing of it.[4] When God says that He has given me something, that something in heaven is mine, I know by faith that it truly is mine.[5] With faith, I am able to believe God when He says that something will come to pass, or that He will do something for me.[6] Faith secures those things that are, but that I have not yet seen, and that are not yet, but will come. "Faith is the substance of things hoped for, the evidence of things not seen" (Hebrews 11:1). Faith always asks only for what God has said, and then relies on His faithfulness and power to fulfill His Word.

Let us review again the words of Scripture. Of Mary we read, "Blessed is she that believed; for there

---

[2]Gen. 21:1; 32:12; Num. 14:17,18,20; Josh. 21:45; 23:14; 2 Sam. 7:25,29; Ps. 119:49
[3]Luke 1:38,45; John 3:33; 4:50; 11:40; 20:29; Heb. 11:11,18
[4]Rom. 1:17; 4:5; 5:1; Gal. 3:27; Eph. 1:19; 3:17
[5]John 3:16,17,36; 1 John 5:12,13
[6]Rom. 8:38; Phil. 3:21; 1 Thess. 5:24; 1 Pet. 1:4,5

shall be a performance of the things which were told her from the Lord." All things that have been spoken in the Word will be fulfilled for me. Therefore, I believe them.

It is reported that Abraham was fully assured that God would fulfill what He had promised him. This is the assurance of faith—to be assured that God will do what He has promised.

It is written in the Word about Paul, "I believe God, that it shall be even as it was told me." It stood fixed with him that God would do what He had spoken.

Young disciples in Christ, the new and eternal life in you is a life of faith. And do you not see how simple and blessed that life of faith is? Every day I go to the Word and hear what God has said that He has done and will do.[7] I take time to house in my heart the Word in which God says that. I hold it firmly, entirely assured that what God has promised He is able to perform. And then, in a childlike spirit, I await the fulfillment of all the promises of His Word. And my soul experiences—Blessed is she that believed, for the things that have been spoken to her from the Lord will be fulfilled. God promises—I believe—God fulfills. That is the secret of the new life.

Father, Your child thanks You for this blessed life of faith in which we have to walk. I can do nothing, but You can do all. All that You can do has been spoken in Your Word. Every Word that I take and trustfully bring to You is fulfilled. Father, in this life of faith, so simple, so glorious, I will walk with You. Amen.

---

[7]Gal. 2:20; 3:2,5; 5:5,6, Heb. 10:35; 1 Pet. 1:3

Notes

1. The Christian must read and search the Scriptures to increase his knowledge. For this reason, he reads one or more principal passages daily. He reads the Scriptures to also strengthen his faith. To achieve this he must take one or two verses and make them the subject of special reflection.

2. Do not allow yourselves to be led astray by those who speak of faith as something great and unintelligible. Faith is nothing more than the certainty that God speaks the truth. Take some promises of God and say to Him, "I know for certain that this promise is truth, and that You will fulfill it." He *will* do it.

3. Never mourn over unbelief as if it were a weakness which you cannot help. As God's child, however weak you may be, you have the power to believe because the Spirit of God is in you. Keep this in mind—no one understands anything unless he has the power to believe. He must simply begin and continue to say to the Lord that he is sure that His Word is truth. He must securely hold the promise and trust God for the fulfillment.

Chapter 5
The Power Of God's Word

"Faith cometh by hearing, and hearing by the word of God" Romans 10:17.

"Receive with meekness the engrafted word, which is able to save your souls" James 1:21.

"We also thank God without ceasing, because when ye received the word of God, which ye heard of us, ye received it not as the word of men, but, as it is in truth, the word of God, which effectively worketh also in you that believe" 1 Thessalonians 2:13.

"For the word of God is quick and powerful" Hebrews 4:12.

The new life of a child of God depends so much on the correct usage of God's Word, that I will once again speak of it with my young brothers and sisters in the Lord.

It is a great thing when the Christian realizes that he can receive and accomplish all only through faith. He has to believe. God will look to the fulfilling of what is promised. Every morning the Christian must trust in Jesus and in the new life given to him. Jesus will see to it that the new life works in him.

But now he runs the risk of another error. He thinks that the faith that does such great things must be something great—that he must have a great power in order to exercise such a great faith.[1] Because he does not feel this power, he thinks that he

---

[1] Luke 17:5,6; Rom. 10:6-8

30

cannot believe as he should. This error may prove to be a loss to him throughout his life.

Hear how distorted this thought is. You must not bring this mighty faith to get the Word fulfilled. Instead, the Word comes and brings you this faith which you must have. "The word is quick and powerful." The Word works faith in you. The Scripture says, "Faith is by the word."

Think on what we have said of the heart as a temple—of its two divisions. There is the outer court, with understanding as its gate or entrance. There is the innermost sanctuary, with the faith of the heart as its entrance. There is a natural faith—the historic faith—which every man has. It is with this that I must first receive the Word into my keeping and my consideration. I must say to myself, "The Word of God is certainly true. I can stand upon it." In this way, I bring the Word into the outer court. From *within* the heart, desire reaches out to the Word, seeking to receive it *into* the heart. The Word now exercises its divine power of life. It begins to grow and shoot out roots. As a seed in the earth sends forth roots and presses still deeper into the soil, the Word presses inwardly into the holy place. The Word thus works true saving faith.[2]

Young Christian, please understand this—the Word is living and powerful. Through the Word you are born again. The Word works faith in you. Through the Word comes faith. Receive the Word simply, with the thought that it will work in you. Keep yourselves occupied with the Word and give it time. The Word has a divine life in itself. Carry it in

---

[2] Thess. 2:13; Jas. 1:21; 1 Pet. 1:23

your innermost parts, and it will work life in you. It will work in you a strong faith, able for anything.

Be resolved never to say, I cannot believe. You *can* believe. You have the Spirit of God in you. Even the natural man can say, "This Word of God is certainly true or certainly not true." If, with desire in your soul, you say, "It is true. I will believe it," the living Spirit—through whom the Word is living and powerful—will work this living faith. Besides, the Spirit is not only in the Word, but is also in you. Although you do not feel as if you were believing, know for certain that you can believe.[3] Begin to actually receive the Word. It will work a mighty faith in you. Depend on God's Word, it can surely be trusted to work faith in you as you receive it.

And not only the promises, but also the commands, have this living power. When I first receive a command from God, I do not feel the power to accomplish it. If I simply receive the Word as God's Word, and trust in its workings, the commandment will work in me the desire and power for obedience. God's Word works for those who believe. When I weigh and firmly hold the command, it works the desire and the will to obey. It strongly urges me toward the conviction that I can certainly do what my Father says. The Word works both faith and obedience. The obedience of the Christian is the obedience of faith. I must believe that through the Spirit I have the power to do what God wills. In the Word, the power of God works in me. The Word, as the command of the living God who loves me, is my power.[4]

---

[3]Deut. 32:46,47; Josh. 1:7,9
[4]Gal. 6:6; 1 Thess. 1:3; Jas. 1:21

Therefore, my young disciples in Christ, learn to receive God's Word trustfully. Even though at first you do not understand it, continue to meditate on it. It has a living power in it, and it will glorify itself. Although you feel no power to believe or to obey, the Word is living and powerful. Take it and hold it fast. It will accomplish its work with divine power. The Word inspires and strengthens our faith and obedience.

Lord God, I begin to conceive how You are in Your Word with Your life and power, and how that Word itself works faith and obedience in the heart that receives and keeps it. Lord, teach me to carry Your every Word as a living seed in my heart, in the assurance that it will work in me all Your good pleasure. Amen.

Notes

1. Do not forget that it is one and the same to believe in the Word, or in the person who speaks the Word, or in the thing which is promised in the Word. The very same faith that receives the promises also receives the Father who promises, and the Son with the salvation that is given in the promises. Please see to it that you never separate the Word and the living God from each other.

2. Also, see to it that you thoroughly understand the distinction between the reception of the Word as the "word of man" and as the "Word of God, which works in you that believe."

3. I think you now know what is necessary to become strong in faith. Exercise as much faith as you have. Take a promise of God. Say to yourself that it is certainly true. Go to God and say to Him that you rely on Him for the fulfillment. Ponder the

promise, and cleave to it in conversation with God. Rely on Him to do for you what He says. He will surely do it.

4. The Spirit and the Word always go together. I can be sure concerning all of what the Word says— that I must do it and can do it through the Spirit. I must receive the Word, and also the command, in the confidence that it is the living Word of the living God which works in us who believe.

Chapter 6
God's Gift Of His Son

"For God so loved the world, that He gave His only begotten Son, that whosoever believeth in Him should not perish, but have everlasting life" John 3:16.

"Thanks be unto God for His unspeakable gift" 2 Corinthians 9:15.

God held the world so dear that He gave His only begotten Son for everyone who will trust in Him. And how did He give Him? He gave Him in His birth as man, in order to be forever one with us. He gave Him in His death on the cross as surety, in order to take away our sin and curse. He gave Him on the throne of heaven, in order to arrange for our welfare, as our Representative and Intercessor over all the powers of heaven. He gave Him in the outpouring of the Spirit, in order to dwell in us—to be entirely and altogether our own.[1] Yes, that is the love of God. He gave His Son to us, for us, and in us.

Nothing less than His Son Himself. This is the love of God. It is not that He gives us something, but that He gives us Someone—a living person—not one or another blessing, but Him, who is all life and blessing—Jesus Himself. He does not simply give us forgiveness, revival, sanctification, or glory—He gives us His own Son, Jesus. The Lord Jesus is the

---

[1] John 1:14,16; 14:23; Rom. 5:8; 8:32,34; Eph. 1:22; 3:17; Col. 2:9,10; Heb. 7:24,26; 1 John 4:9,10

beloved, the equal, the bosom friend, the eternal blessedness of the Father. And it is the will of God that we should have Jesus as ours, even as He has Him.[2] For this reason He gave Him to us. The whole of salvation consists of this—to have, to possess, to enjoy Jesus. God has given His Son, given Him wholly to become ours.[3]

What do we have to do? To take Him, to receive and to take possession of the gift—to enjoy Jesus as our own. This is eternal life. "He that hath the Son hath life."[4]

How I wish that all young Christians would understand this. The one great work of God's love for us is, He gives us His Son. In Him we have all. Therefore, the one great work of our heart must be to receive this Jesus who has been given to us, and to consider and use Him as ours. I must begin every day anew with the thought, I have Jesus to do all for me.[5] In all weakness or darkness or danger—in the case of every desire or need—let your first thought always be, I have Jesus to make everything right for me. God has given Him to me for this purpose. Whether your need is forgiveness, consolation, or confirmation, remember, the Father gave you Jesus to care for you. Whether you have fallen, or are tempted to fall, into danger, remember, Jesus has been given to you for your care. Whether you do not know the will of God in one matter or another, or whether you are unsure of your strength and courage to do His will,

[2]Matt. 11:27; John 17:23,25; Rom. 8:38,39; Heb. 2:11
Tim. 1:12
[3]Ps. 73:24; 142:6; John 20:28; Heb. 3:14
[4]John 1:12; 2 Cor. 3:5; Col. 2:6; 1 John 5:12
[5]John 15:5; Rom. 8:37; 1 Cor. 1:30; Eph. 1:3; 2:10; Phil. 4:13; 2

remember, Jesus will care for you.

For this reason, rely every day on this gift from God. It has been presented to you in the Word. Appropriate the Son by faith in the Word. Take Him again every day. Through faith you have the Son.[6] The love of God has given the Son. Take Him and hold Him steadily in the love of your heart.[7] It is to bring life, eternal life, to you that God has given Jesus. Take Him up into your life. Let your heart and tongue and whole walk be under the might and guidance of Jesus.[8]

Young Christian, so weak and so sinful, please listen to that word. God has given you Jesus. He is yours. Taking is nothing else but the fruit of faith. The gift is for you. He will do all for you.

Lord Jesus, today and every day, I take You. In all Your fullness and in all Your relations, without ceasing, I take You for myself. You are my Wisdom, my Light, my Leader. I take You as my Prophet. You, who perfectly reconciles me and brings me near to God, who purifies and sanctifies me and prays for me, I take as my Priest. You, who guides and keeps and blesses me, I take as my King. You, Lord, are all, and You are wholly mine. Thanks be to God for His unspeakable gift. Amen.

Notes

1. Often ponder the word "give." God gives in a wonderful way—from the heart, completely and for nothing—to the unworthy. And He gives effectively. What He gives He will truly make our possession,

---

[6] John 1:12; 1 John 5:9,13
[7] 1 John 4:4,19
[8] 2 Cor. 5:15; Phil. 3:8

inwardly and entirely. Believe this, and you will have the certainty that Jesus will come into your possession with all that He brings.

2. Also ponder the word "take." Our great work is to take Jesus, to hold Him firmly, and to appropriate Him when received. That taking is nothing but trusting. He is mine with all that He has. The secret of the life of faith is to take Jesus—the full Jesus—as yours every day.

3. Let the word "have" weigh heavily with you. "He that hath the Son hath life" (1 John 5:12). What I have is mine, for my use and service. I can have the full enjoyment of it.

4. Especially notice what God gives and what you take. What you have now is nothing less than the living Son of God. Do you receive this?

Chapter 7

Jesus' Surrender Of Himself

"Christ also loved the Church, and gave Himself for it; that He might sanctify and cleanse it; that He might present it to Himself a glorious Church, not having spot or wrinkle; but that it should be holy and without blemish" Ephesians 5:25-27.

Jesus' work for the sinner was so great and wonderful that it was necessary for Him to give Himself on the cross for that work. Jesus' love for us was so great and wonderful that He actually gave Himself for us and to us. Jesus' surrender is so great and wonderful that all which He gave Himself for can be truly and entirely ours. For Jesus, the Holy, the Almighty, has taken it upon Himself to do it. He gave *Himself* for us.[1] And now the one necessary thing is that we should rightly understand and firmly believe in His surrender for us.

To what end, then, was it that He gave Himself for the Church? Hear what God says. The aim of Jesus is that He might sanctify the Church so that it would be without blemish.[2] He will attain His aim in the soul as long as the soul falls into His will, makes His will its most important consideration, and relies on Jesus' surrender of Himself to do so.

Hear this word of God, "Who gave Himself for us, that He might redeem us from all iniquity, and

---

[1]Gal. 1:4; 2:20; Eph. 5:2,25; 1 Tim. 2:6; Tit. 2:14
[2]Eph. 1:4; 5:27; Col. 1:22; 1 Thess. 2:10; 3:13; 5:23,24

purify unto Himself a people for His own possession, zealous of good works" (Titus 2:14). Jesus gave Himself in order to prepare for Himself a *pure* people, a people *of His own*, a *zealous* people. When I receive Him, and when I believe that He gave Himself for me, I will certainly experience it. I will be purified through Him. I will be held securely as His possession and be filled with zeal and joy to work for Him.

And notice how the operation of this surrender of Himself will result in His having us entirely for Himself—"that He might present us to Himself," "that He might purify us to Himself, a people of His own." The more I understand and contemplate Jesus' surrender of Himself for me, the more I give myself again to Him. The surrender is a mutual one—the love comes from both sides. His giving of Himself makes such an impression on my heart, that my heart, with the self-same love and joy, becomes entirely His. Through giving Himself to me, He takes possession of me. He becomes mine and I become His. I know that I have Jesus wholly for me, and that He has me wholly for Himself.[3]

And how do I come to the full enjoyment of this blessed life? "I live by the faith of the Son of God, who loved me and gave Himself for me" (Galatians 2:20).[4] Through faith, I reflect on and contemplate His surrender to me as sure and glorious. Through faith, I believe it. Through faith, I trust in Jesus to confirm this surrender, to communicate Himself to me, and to reveal Himself within me. Through faith,

[3]Ex. 19:4,5; Deut. 26:7,18; Isa. 41:9,10; 1 Cor. 6:19,20; 1 Pet. 2:10
[4]John 6:29,35; 7:38; 10:10,38

I await—with certainty—the full experience of salvation which comes from having Jesus as mine, to do all for me. Through faith, I live in Jesus who loved me and gave Himself for me. And I say, "No longer do I live, but Christ liveth in me" (Galatians 2:20). Christian, please believe with your whole heart that Jesus gives Himself for you. He is wholly yours. He will do all for you.[5]

Lord Jesus, what wonderful grace is this, that You gave Yourself for me. In You there is eternal life. You are the life, and You give Yourself to be all that I need in my life. You purify me, sanctify me, and make me zealous in good works. You take me wholly for Yourself, and give Yourself wholly for me. Yes, my Lord, in all You are my life. Make me rightly understand this. Amen.

Notes

1. It was in His great love that the Father gave the Son. It was out of love that Jesus gave Himself (Rom. 3:16; Eph. 5:26). The taking, the having of Jesus, is the entrance into a life in the love of God. This is the highest life (John 14:21,28; 17:23,26; Eph. 3:17,18). Through faith we must press into love and live there (1 John 4:16-18).

2. Do you think that you have now learned all the lesson and how to begin every day with a childlike trust? I take Jesus this day to be my life and to do all for me.

3. Understand that to take and to have Jesus presupposes a personal communion with Him. To

---

[5]Matt. 8:10; 9:2,22; Mark 11:24; Luke 7:50; 8:48; 17:19; 18:42; Rom. 4:20,21; 5:2; 11:20; Gal. 3:25,26; Eph. 1:19; 3:17

have pleasure in Him, to gladly hold conversation with Him, to rejoice in Him as my friend and in His love—this leads to the faith that truly takes Him.

Chapter 8
Children Of God

"As many as received Him, to them gave He the power to become children of God, even to them that believe on His name" John 1:12.

What is given must be received, otherwise it does not profit. If the first great deed of God's love is the gift of His Son, then the first work of man must be to receive this Son. And if all the blessings of God's love come to us only in the ever-new, ever-living Son of the Father, then all these blessings enter into us daily through the always new, always continuing reception of the Son.

You, beloved young Christians, know what is necessary for this reception because you have already received the Lord Jesus. But all that this reception involves must become clearer and stronger—the unceasing, living action of your faith.[1] Within this action lies the increase of faith. Your first receiving of Jesus rested on the certainty provided by the Word—that He was for you. Through the Word your soul must be further filled with the assurance that all that is in Him is literally and truly for you, given to you by the Father; He is to be your life.

The impulse to your first receiving was based on your want and necessity. Now, through the Spirit, you become still poorer in spirit, and you see how

---

[1] 2 Cor. 10:15; 1 Thess. 1:8; 3:10; 2 Thess. 1:3

much you have need of Jesus for everything, every moment. This leads to a ceaseless, ever-active taking of Him as your all.[2]

When you first received, it was by faith in that which you could not yet see or feel. That same faith must be continually exercised in saying, "All that I see in Jesus is for me. I take it as mine, although I do not yet experience it." The love of God is a communicating—a ceaseless outstreaming of His light of life over the soul. It is a very powerful and genuine giving of Jesus. Our life is nothing but a continuous blessed understanding and reception of Him.[3]

And this is the way to live as children of God. To as many as receive Him, to them He gives the power to become children of God. This holds true, not only of conversion and regeneration, but also every day of my life. If to walk in all things as a child of God and to exhibit the image of my Father is indispensable, then I must take Jesus, the only begotten Son. It is He who makes me a child of God. The way to live as a child of God is to have the heart and life full of Jesus. I go to the Word to learn all the characteristics of a child of God.[4] After each one of them I write—"Jesus will work in me; I have *Him* to help me to be a child of God."

Beloved young Christian, I implore you to learn to understand the simplicity and the glory of being a true Christian. It is to receive Jesus in all His fullness and in all the glorious relations in which the Father gives Him to you. Take Him as your Prophet, as

---

[2]Matt. 5:3; 1 Cor. 3:10,13,16; Eph. 4:14,15; Col. 2:6
[3]John 1:16; Col. 2:9,10; 3:3
[4]Matt. 5:9,16,44,45; Rom. 8:14; Eph. 1:4,5; 5:1,2; Phil. 2:15; Heb. 2:10; 1 Pet. 1:14,17; 1 John 3:1,10; 5:1,3

your wisdom, your light, your guide. Take Him as your Priest, who renews you, purifies you, sanctifies you, brings you near to God, takes you, and forms you wholly for His service. Take Him as your King, who governs you, protects you, and blesses you. Take Him as your Head, your example, your Brother, your life, your all. The giving of God is a divine and an ever-progressive, effectual communication to your soul. Let your taking be the childlike, cheerful, continuous opening of mouth and heart for what God gives—the full Jesus and all His grace. To every prayer the answer of God is Jesus. All is in Him, and all in Him is for you. Let your response always be, "Jesus, in Him I have all." You are and you live, in all things, as children of God through faith in Jesus.

Father, open the eyes of my heart to understand what it is to be a child of God and to live always as a child, through always believing in Jesus, Your only Son. Let every breath of my soul be faith in Jesus, a confidence in Him, a resting in Him, a surrender to Him, so that He may work all in me. Amen.

Notes

1. By the grace of God, you now know that you have received Jesus and are God's child; you must now take pains to make His salvation known. There is many a one who longs to know and cannot find out how he can become a child of God.

2. Endeavor to make two things plain to him. First, that the new birth is something so high and holy that he can do nothing in it. He must receive eternal life from God through the Spirit. He must be born from above. This Jesus teaches (John 3:1-8).

Then, make it clear to him how low God has descended to us with this new life, and how near He brings it to us. In Jesus there is life for everyone who believes in Him. This Jesus teaches (John 3:14-18). And Jesus and the life are in the Word.

3. Tell the sinner that when he takes the Word, he then has Jesus and life in the Word (Rom. 10:8). Take pains to tell the glad tidings that we become children of God only through faith in Jesus.

Chapter 9

Our Surrender To Jesus

"They gave their own selves to the Lord" 2 Corinthians 8:5.

The chief element of what Jesus has done for me—always does for me—lies in His surrender of Himself for me. I have the main element of what He would have me do in my surrender to Him. For young Christians who have given themselves to Jesus, it is of great importance to always hold fast—to confirm and renew this surrender. This is the special life of faith which says again every day, "I have given myself to Him. I will follow and serve Him.[1] He has taken me. I am His and entirely at His service."[2]

Young Christian, hold firm your surrender and continue to make it firmer. When a stumbling or a sin recurs after you have surrendered yourself, do not think that the surrender was insincere. No, the surrender to Jesus does not make us perfect at once. You have sinned because you were not thoroughly or firmly enough in His arms. Adhere to this, even though it is with shame, "Lord, You know I have given myself to You, and I am Yours."[3] Confirm this surrender again. Say to Him that you now begin to see better how complete the surrender to Him must

[1]Matt. 4:22; 10:24,25,37,38; Luke 18:22; John 12:25,26; 2 Cor. 5:15
[2]Matt. 28:20
[3]John 21:17; Gal. 6:1; 1 Thess. 5:24; 2 Tim. 2:13; 1 John 5:16

be. Every day, renew the voluntary, entire, and undivided offering up of yourselves to Him.[4]

The longer we continue as Christians, the deeper our insight into God's Word will lead us to surrender to Jesus. We will see more clearly that we do not yet fully understand or contemplate it. The surrender must become more undivided and trustful. The language which Ahab once used must be ours, "My Lord, O King, according to thy saying, I am thine, and all that I have" (1 Kings 20:4). This is the language of undivided dedication—I am thine, and all that I have. Keep nothing back. Keep back no single sin that you do not confess and turn from. Without conversion there can be no surrender.[5] Lay upon the altar all of your thoughts, your utterances, your feelings, your labors, your time, your influence, and your property.[6] Jesus has a right to all—He demands the whole. Give yourself, with all that you have, to be guided and used and kept, undivided and blessed. "My Lord, O King, according to thy saying, I am thine, and all that I have."

That is the language of trustful dedication. It is on the Word of the Lord—which calls upon you to surrender yourself—that you have done this. That Word is your guarantee that He will take and guide and keep you. As surely as you give yourself does He take you. And what He takes He can keep. Only we must not take it out of His hand again. Let it remain fixed with you, that your surrender is in the highest degree pleasing to Him. Be assured of it, your offering is a sweet smelling savor. Not on what you are or

---

[4]Luke 18:28; Phil. 3:7,8
[5]Matt. 7:21; John 3:20,21; 2 Tim. 2:19,21
[6]Rom. 6:13,22; 12:1; 2 Cor. 5:15; Heb. 13:15; 1 Pet. 2:5

what you experience or discover in yourselves do you say this, but on His Word. According to His Word you are able to stand on this—what you give He will take, and what He takes He will keep.[7] Therefore, every day let this be the childlike joyful activity of your life of faith. Surrender yourselves continually to Jesus, and you are safe in the certainty that He, in His love, takes and holds you securely. His answer to your giving is the renewed and always deeper surrender of Himself to you.

According to Your Word, my Lord and King, I am Yours, and all that I have. Every day, this day, I will confirm it. I am not my own, but am my Lord's. Fervently I implore You to take full possession of Your property so that no one may doubt whose I am. Amen.

Notes

1. Ponder once again the words *giving* and *taking* and *having*. What I give to Jesus, He takes with a divine taking. And what He takes, He has and thereafter cares for. Now it is absolutely no longer mine. I must have no thought of it. I may not dispose of it. Let your faith find full expression in adoration. Jesus takes me. Jesus has me.

2. Should a time of doubting or darkness overtake you, and your assurance that the Lord has received you has come to be lost, do not allow yourself to become discouraged. Come simply as a sinner and confess your sins. Believe in His promises that He will by no means cast out those who come to Him, and begin simply on the ground of the promises to say, "I know that He has received me."

---

[7]John 10:28; 2 Thess. 3:3; 2 Tim. 1:12

3. Do not forget what the chief element in surrender is—it is a surrender to Jesus and to His love. Fix your eye not on your activity in surrender, but on Jesus who calls you, who takes you, and who can do all for you. This is what makes faith strong.

4. Faith is always a surrender. Faith is the eye for seeing the invisible. When I look at something, I surrender myself to the impression which it makes upon me. Faith is the ear that hearkens to the voice of God. When I believe a message, I surrender myself to the influence, whether cheering or saddening, which the words exercise on me. When I believe in Jesus, I surrender myself to Him, in reflection, in desire, in expectation, in order that He may *be* in me and *do* in me that for which He has been given to me by God.

Chapter 10
A Savior From Sin

"Thou shalt call His name Jesus; for He shall save His people from their sins" Matthew 1:21.

"Ye know that He was manifest to take away sins; and in Him is no sin. Whosoever abideth in Him sinneth not" 1 John 3:5,6.

It is sin that is the cause of our misery. It is sin that provoked God and brought His curse on man. He hates sin with a perfect hatred and will do everything to root it out.[1] It is to take away sin that God gave His Son—that Jesus gave Himself.[2] It is God who sets us free. Not only free from punishment, curse, uneasiness and terror, but also free from sin itself.[3] You know that He was manifested so that He might take away our sins. Let us receive this thought deep into our hearts—it is God who takes away our sins. The better we grasp this the more blessed our life will be.

All do not receive this. They chiefly seek to be freed from the consequences of sin, from fear and darkness, and the punishment that sin brings.[4] It is for this reason that they do not come to the true rest of salvation. They do not understand that to be saved is to be freed from sin. Let us hold it firmly.

---

[1]Deut. 27:26; Isa. 59:1,2; Jer. 44:4; Rom. 1:18
[2]Gal. 2:4; Eph. 5:25,27; 1 Pet. 2:24; 1 John 3:3,8
[3]Jer. 27:9; 1 Pet. 1:2,15,16; 2:14; 1 John 3:8
[4]Gen. 27:34; Isa. 58:5,6; John 6:26; Jas. 4:3

Jesus saves through the taking away of sin. Then we will learn two things.

The first is to come to Jesus with every sin.[5] Now that you have given yourself over to the Lord, do not lose heart over the sin which still attacks and rules you. Make no endeavor to take away and overcome sin merely by your own strength. Bring every sin to Jesus. He has been ordained by God to take away sin. He has already brought it to nothingness upon the cross and has broken its power.[6] It is His work— it is His desire—to set you free from it. Learn, then, to always come to Jesus with every sin. Sin is your deadly foe. If you confess it to Jesus—surrender it to Him—you will certainly overcome it.[7]

Learn to believe this firmly. This is the second point. Understand that Jesus Himself is the Savior from sin. It is not *you* who must overcome sin with the help of Jesus, but Jesus Himself—Jesus in you.[8] If, in this way, you become free from sin and enjoy full salvation, then endeavor to always stand in full fellowship with Jesus. Do not wait until you enter into temptation to ask for the help of Jesus. But let your life beforehand always be through Jesus. Let His nearness be your one desire. Jesus saves from sin, and to have Jesus is salvation from sin.[9] O that we could rightly understand this! The saving from sin is not an occasional event, but, rather, it is a blessing through Jesus, to us and in us.[10] When Jesus fills me, when Jesus is all for me, sin has no hold on

---

[5]Ps. 32:5; Luke 7:38; 19:7,8,10; John 8:11
[6]Heb. 9:26
[7]Rom. 7:4,9; 8:2; 2 Cor. 12:9; 2 Thess. 2:3
[8]Deut. 8:17,18; Ps. 44:4; John 16:33; 1 John 5:4,5
[9]1 Cor. 15:10; Gal. 2:20; Phil. 4:13; Col. 3:3-5
[10]Ex. 29:43; John 15:4,5; Rom. 8:10; Eph. 3:17,18

me. "Whosoever abideth in Him sinneth not."

Yes, sin is driven out and kept out only through the presence of Jesus. It is Jesus Himself, through His giving to me and His living in me, who is my salvation from sin.

Precious Lord, let Your light stream over me. Let it become clearer to my soul that You Yourself are my salvation. To have You with me, in me—this keeps sin out. Teach me to bring every sin to You. Let every sin drive me to a closer alliance with You. Then Your name will truly become my salvation from sin. Amen.

Notes

1. See of what importance it is that the Christian should always grow in the knowledge of sin. The sin that I do not know, I cannot bring to Jesus. The sin that I do not bring to Him is not taken out of me.

2. To know sin better the following things are required:

—The constant prayer, "Examine me; make known to me my transgression and my sin" (Job 13:23; Ps. 139:23,24).

—A tender conscience that is willing to be convinced of sin through the Spirit, as He also uses the conscience for this end.

—The very humble surrender to the Word, to think about sin only as God thinks.

3. The deeper knowledge of sin will be found in these results:

—That we will see as sin things which we previously did not regard in this light.

—That we will more exceedingly perceive the detestable character of sin (Rom. 7:13).

—That with the overcoming of external sins we

come to understand more clearly the deep sinfulness of our nature, of the enmity of our flesh against God. Then we give up all hope of being or of doing anything good, and we are turned wholly to live in faith through the Spirit.

4. Let us thank God very heartily that Jesus is a Savior from sin. The power that sin has had over us, Jesus now has. The place that sin has taken in the heart, Jesus will now take. "The law of the Spirit of life in Christ Jesus hath made me free from the law of sin and death" (Rom. 8:2).

Chapter 11

The Confession Of Sin

"If we confess our sins, He is faithful and just to forgive us our sins, and to cleanse us from all unrighteousness" 1 John 1:9.

The one thing which God hates is sin. It grieves and provokes Him, and He *will* destroy it. The one thing that makes man unhappy is sin.[1] The one thing which Jesus had to give His blood for was sin. In all the communication between the sinner and God, this is the first thing which the sinner must bring to his God—sin.[2]

When you first came to Jesus, you perceived this in some measure. But you should learn to understand this lesson more deeply. The one counsel concerning sin is—bring it daily to the only One who can take it away, God Himself. You should learn that one of the greatest privileges of a child of God is the confession of sin. It is only the holiness of God that can consume sin. Through confession I must hand over my sin to God, lay it down in God, and get God's acquittal of it. I must cast it into the fiery oven of God's holy love which burns against sin like a fire. God, yes, God Himself, and He alone, takes away sin.[3]

---

[1]Gen. 6:5,6; Isa. 43:24; Ezek. 33:6; Rev. 6:16,17
[2]Judg. 10:10,15,16; Ezra 9:6; Neh. 9:2,33; Jer. 3:21,25; Dan. 9:4,5,20
[3]Lev. 6:21; Num. 5:7; 2 Sam. 12:13; Ps. 32:5; 38:18; 51:5,19

The Christian does not always understand this. He has an inborn tendency to want to cover sin, or to make it less, or to root it out only when he desires to draw near to God. He considers covering the sin with repentance, self-blame, or with contempt for the temptation which caused him to sin. He tries to conceal sin with the fruits of the works he has done or still hopes to do.[4] Young Christian, if you want to enjoy the peacefulness of a complete forgiveness and a divine cleansing of sin, see to it that you correctly use the confession of sin. In the true confession of sin, you have one of the most blessed privileges of a child of God, and one of the deepest roots of a powerful spiritual life.

For this end, let your confession be a precise one.[5] The continued, uncertain confession of sin does more harm than good. It is much better to say to God, "I have nothing to confess," than to say, "I do not know what to confess." Begin with one sin. Let it come to a complete harmony between God and you concerning this one sin. Let it be fixed with you that this sin is—through confession—placed in God's hands. You will experience that in such confessions there is both power and blessing.

Let the confession be a righteous one.[6] Deliver up the sinful deed to be laid aside. Deliver up the sinful feeling with trust in the Lord. Confession implies renunciation—the putting off of sin. Give up sin to God, who forgives you of it, and cleanses you from it. Do not confess, if you are not prepared, or if you

---

[4]Gen. 3:12; Ex. 32:22,24; Isa. 1:11,5; Luke 13:26
[5]Num. 12:11; 21:7; 2 Sam. 24:10,17; Isa. 59:12,13; Luke 23:41; Acts 19:18,19; 22:19,20; 1 Tim. 1:13,15
[6]Prov. 28:13; Lev. 26:40,41; Jer. 31:18,19

do not heartily desire to be freed from it. Confession has value only if it is a giving up of sin to God.

Let the confession be one of trust.[7] Depend entirely on God to actually forgive you, and to cleanse you from sin. Continue in confession by casting the sin you desire to be rid of into the fire of God's holiness until your soul has the firm confidence that God takes it on His own account to forgive and to cleanse. It is this faith which truly overcomes the world and sin. It is the faith that God, in Jesus, actually frees us from sin.[8]

Brothers and sisters, do you understand it now? What must you do with sin, with every sin? Bring it in confession to God, and give it to God. God alone takes away sin.

Lord God, what thanks I will express for this unspeakable blessing—that I may come to You with sin. It is known to You, Lord, how sin before Your holiness causes terror and flight. It is known to You how it is our deepest thought, first to have sin covered, and then to come to You with our desire and endeavor for good. Lord, teach me to come to You with sin—every sin—and in confession to lay it down before You and give it up to You. Amen.

Notes

1. What is the distinction between the covering of sin by God and by man? How does man do it? How does God do it?

2. What are the great hindrances in the way of the confession of sin?

—Ignorance about sin,

---

[7] 2 Sam. 12:13; Ps. 32:5; Isa. 55:7
[8] 1 John 5:5

—Fear to come with sin to the Holy Father,

—The endeavor to come to God with something good,

—Unbelief in the power of the blood of Jesus and in the riches of grace.

3. Must I immediately confess an oath or a lie or a wrong word, or wait until my feeling has first cooled and become correctly disposed? Confess it immediately; come in full sinfulness to God, without first desiring to make it less!

4. Is it also necessary to confess before man? It is indispensable if our sin has been against man. Also, we must be careful, for it is often easier to acknowledge a wrong before God than before man (Jas. 5:16).

Chapter 12
The Forgiveness of Sins

"Blessed is he whose transgression is forgiven, whose sin is covered" Psalm 32:1.

"Bless the Lord, O my soul....who forgiveth all thine inquities" Psalm 103:2,3.

In connection with surrender to the Lord, it was said that the first great blessing of the grace of God was this—the free, complete, everlasting forgiveness of all your sins. For the young Christian, it is of great importance that he should stand firm in this forgiveness of his sins. He should always carry the certainty of it about with him. For this reason, he must especially consider the following truths.

The forgiveness of our sin is a complete forgiveness.[1] God does not partially forgive. Even with man, we believe that half forgiveness is not true forgiveness. The love of God is so great, and the atonement in the blood of Jesus so complete and powerful, that God always forgives completely. Take time with God's Word so that you may fully understand that your guilt has been blotted out completely. God absolutely thinks no more about your sins. "I will forgive their iniquity, and I will remember their sin no more."[2]

The forgiveness of our sin restores us entirely

---

[1]Ps. 103:12; Isa. 38:17; 55:7; Mic. 7:18,19; Heb. 10:16-18
[2]Jer. 31:34; Heb. 8:12; 10:17

again to the love of God.[3] Not only does God no longer attribute us with sin, but He also restores us to the righteousness of Jesus—for His sake we are as dear to God as He is. Not only is wrath turned away from us, but the fullness of love now rests upon us. "I will love them freely: for mine anger is turned away from him" (Hosea 14:4). Forgiveness is the access to all of God's love. On this account, forgiveness is also an introduction to all the other blessings of redemption.

Live in the full assurance of forgiveness, and let the Spirit fill your heart with the certainty and the blessedness of it. Then you will have great confidence in expecting all from God. Learn from the Word of God—through the Spirit—to know God correctly, and to trust Him as the ever-forgiving God. That is His name and His glory. To one to whom much, yes, all is forgiven, He will also give much. He will give all.[4] Therefore, let it be your joyful thanksgiving every day. "Bless the Lord, O my soul, who forgiveth all thine iniquities." Then forgiveness becomes the power of a new life. "Her sins which are many, are forgiven: for she loved much" (Luke 7:47). The forgiveness of sins, received in living faith every day, is a bond which binds you to Jesus and His service.[5]

Then, the forgiveness of former sins supplies the courage to immediately confess every new sin and to trustfully receive forgiveness.[6] Look, however, to

---

[3]Hos. 14:5; Luke 15:22; Acts 26:18; Rom. 5:1,5

[4]Ps. 103:3; Isa. 12:1,3; Rom. 5:10; 8:32; Eph. 1:7; 3:5

[5]John 13:14,15; Rom. 12:1; 1 Cor. 6:20; Eph. 5:25,26; Tit. 2:14; 1 Pet. 1:17,18

[6]Ex. 34:6,7; Matt. 18:21; Luke 1:77,78

one thing—the certainty of forgiveness must not be a matter of memory or understanding, but must be the fruit of life. It must be our living relationship with the forgiving Father and with Jesus in whom we have forgiveness.[7] It is not enough to know that I once received forgiveness. My life in the love of God, my living communion with Jesus by faith—this makes the forgiveness of sin again always new and powerful. It is the joy and the life of my soul.

Lord God, this is the wonder of Your grace—that You are a forgiving God. Teach me every day to know in this the glory of Your love. Let the Holy Spirit seal forgiveness to me as a blessing, everlasting, ever-fresh, living, and powerful. And let my life be like a song of thanksgiving. "Bless the Lord, O my soul, who forgiveth all thine iniquities." Amen.

Notes

1. Forgiveness is one with justification. Forgiveness is the word that looks more to the relation of God as Father. Justification looks more to His acquittal as Judge. Forgiveness is a word that is more easily understood by the young Christian. But he must also endeavor to understand the word justification and to become familiar with all that the Scriptures teach about it.

2. About justification we must understand:

—That man in himself is totally unrighteous;

—That he cannot be justified by works, that is, pronounced righteous before the judgment seat of the Father;

—That Christ Jesus has brought righteousness for our sake. His obedience is our righteousness;

[7]Eph. 2:13,18; Phil. 3:9; Col. 1:21,22

—That we, through faith, receive Him, are united with Him, and then are pronounced righteous before God;

—That we, through faith, have the certainty of this, and, as justified, draw near to God;

—That union with Jesus is a life by which we are not only pronounced righteous, but are truly righteous and act righteously.

3. Let the certainty of your part in justification, in the full forgiveness of your sins, and full restoration to the love of God, be your confidence in drawing near to God every day.

Chapter 13
The Cleansing Of Sin

"If we walk in the light, the blood of Jesus His Son cleanseth us from all sin. If we confess our sins, He is faithful and just to forgive us our sins, and to cleanse us from all unrighteousness" 1 John 1:7,9.

The same God who forgives sin also cleanses from it. Cleansing is no less a promise of God than is forgiveness; therefore, it is a matter of faith. Cleansing, as well as forgiveness, is as obtainable from God as it is indispensable and impossible for man.

And what now is this cleansing? The word comes from the Old Testament. While forgiveness was a sentence of acquittal passed on the sinner, cleansing was something that happened to him and in him. Forgiveness came to him through the Word. Cleansing was something done to him that he could experience.[1] Consequently, we are liberated from unrighteousness and from the pollution and the working of sin by the inner revelation of the power of God—cleansing. Through cleansing we obtain the blessing of a pure heart—a heart in which the Spirit can complete His operations with a view to sanctifying us and revealing God within us.[2]

Forgiveness and cleansing are both through the blood of Jesus. The blood breaks the power that sin

---

[1]Lev. 13:13; 14:7,8; Num. 19:12; 31:23,24; 2 Sam. 22:21,25; Neh. 13:30; Mal. 3:3

[2]Ps. 51:12; 73:1; Matt. 5:8; 1 Tim. 1:5; 2 Tim. 2:22; 1 Pet. 1:22

has in heaven to condemn us. The blood also breaks the power of sin in the heart which holds us captive. The blood has a ceaseless operation in heaven from moment to moment. The blood has likewise a ceaseless operation in our heart—to purify the heart from the sin which always seeks to penetrate from the flesh. The blood cleanses the conscience from dead works, to serve the living God. The marvelous power that the blood has in heaven, it also has in the heart.[3]

Cleansing is also through the Word—the Word testifies of the blood and of the power of God.[4] Therefore, cleansing is also through faith. It is a divine and effectual cleansing, but it must be received in faith before it can be experienced and felt. I believe that I am cleansed with a divine cleansing, even while I still perceive sin in the flesh. Through faith in this blessing, cleansing itself will be my daily experience.

Cleansing is sometimes ascribed to God, or to the Lord Jesus, or sometimes to man.[5] That is because God cleanses us by making us active in our own cleansing. Through the blood, the lust which leads to sin is mortified, the certainty of power against sin is awakened, and the desire and the will are thus made alive. Happy is the person who understands this. He is protected against the useless pursuit of self-purification in his own strength, because he knows God alone can do it. He is protected against discouragement, for he knows God will certainly do it.

Accordingly, our chief emphasis occurs in two

---

[3]John 13:10,11; Heb. 9:14; 10:22; 1 John 1:7
[4]John 15:3
[5]Ps. 51:3; Ezek. 30:25; John 13:2; 2 Cor. 7:1; 1 Tim. 5:22; 2 Tim. 2:21; Jas. 4:8; 1 John 3:8

things—the desire and the reception of cleansing. The desire must be strong for a real purification. Forgiveness must be only the gateway or beginning of a holy life. I have remarked several times that the secret of progress in the service of God is a strong yearning to become free from every sin—a hunger and thirst after righteousness.[6] Blessed are they who thus yearn. They will understand and receive the promise of a cleansing through God.

They also learn what it means to do this in faith. Through faith they know that an unseen, spiritual, heavenly, but very real cleansing through the blood is being worked in them by God Himself.

Child of God, you remember how we have seen that it was to cleanse us that Jesus gave Himself.[7] Let Him, the Lord God, cleanse you. Having these promises of a divine cleansing, receive this cleansing for yourself. Believe that every sin, when it is forgiven you, is also cleansed away. It will be to you according to your faith. Let your faith in God, in the Word, in the blood, in your Jesus, continually increase. "God is faithful and just to cleanse us from all unrighteousness."

Lord God, I thank You for these promises. You not only give forgiveness, but also cleansing. As surely as forgiveness comes first, does cleansing follow for everyone who desires it and believes. Lord, let Your Word penetrate my heart, and let a divine cleansing from every sin that is forgiven me be the continual expectation of my soul.

Beloved Savior, let the glorious, ceaseless cleans-

---

[6]Ps. 19:13; Matt. 5:6
[7]Eph. 5:26; Tit. 2:14

*ing of Your blood, through Your Spirit in me, be
made known to me and shared by me every moment.
Amen.*

Notes

1. What is the connection between cleansing by
God and cleansing by man himself?

2. What, according to 1 John 1:9, are the two
things that must precede cleansing?

3. Is cleansing, as well as forgiveness, the work of
God in us? If this is the case, of what inexpressible
importance is it to trust God for it? To believe that
God gives me a divine cleansing in the blood when
He forgives me is the way to become partaker of it.

4. What, according to Scripture, are the evidences
of a pure heart?

5. What are "clean hands" (Ps. 24:4)?

Chapter 14

Holiness

"But as He which hath called you is holy, so be ye holy in all manner of conversation: because it is written, Be ye holy; for I am holy" 1 Peter 1:15,16.

"But of Him are ye in Christ Jesus, who of God is made unto us sanctification" 1 Corinthians 1:30.

"God hath from the beginning chosen you unto salvation through sanctification of the Spirit and belief of the truth" 2 Thessalonians 2:13.

Not only has God chosen and called us for salvation, but also for holiness—salvation in holiness. The goal of the young Christian must not only be safety in Christ, but also holiness in Christ. Safety and salvation are, in the long run, found only in holiness. The Christian who thinks that his salvation consists merely in safety and not in holiness will find himself deceived. Young Christian, listen to the Word of God—Be ye holy.

And why must I be holy? Because He who called you is holy and summons you to fellowship and conformity with Himself. How can anyone be saved in God when he does not have the same disposition as God?[1]

God's holiness is His highest glory. In His holiness, His righteousness and His love are united. His holiness is the flaming fire of His zeal against all that

---

[1] Ex.19:6; Lev. 11:44; 19:2; 20:6,7

[2] Ex. 15:11; Isa. 12:6; 41:14; 43:15; 49:7; Hos. 11:9

is sin. This is how He keeps Himself free from sin, and in love makes others also free from it. It is as the Holy One of Israel that He is the Redeemer, and that He lives in the midst of His people.[2] Redemption is given to bring us to Himself and to the fellowship of His holiness. We cannot possibly take part in the love and salvation of God if we are not holy as He is holy.[3] Young Christians, be holy.

And what is this holiness that I must have? Christ is your sanctification. The life of Christ in you is your holiness.[4] In Christ you are sanctified—you are holy. In Christ you must continually be sanctified. The glory of Christ must penetrate your whole life.

Holiness is more than purity. In Scripture we see that cleansing precedes holiness.[5] Cleansing is the taking away of that which is wrong—liberation from sin. Holiness is the filling with that which is good and divine—the disposition of Jesus. Holiness is conformity to Him. It is separation from the spirit of the world and being filled with the presence of the Holy God. The tabernacle was holy because God lived there. We are holy, as God's temple, after we have God living within us. Christ's life in us is our holiness.[6]

And how do we become holy? By the sanctification of the Spirit. The Spirit of God is named the Holy Spirit because He makes us holy. He reveals and glorifies Christ in us. Through Him, Christ dwells in us, and His holy power works in us. Through this Holy Spirit, the workings of the flesh

---

[3]Isa. 10:17; Heb. 12:14
[4]1 Cor. 1:2; Eph. 5:27
[5]2 Cor. 7:1; Eph. 5:26,27; 2 Tim. 2:21
[6]Ex. 29:43,45; 1 Cor. 1:2; 3:15,17; 6:19

are mortified, and God works in us both the will and the accomplishment.[7]

And what work do we have to do to receive this holiness of Christ through the Holy Spirit? "God hath chosen you to salvation, through sanctification of the Spirit *and belief of the truth*" (2 Thessalonians 2:13). The holiness of Christ becomes ours through faith. Naturally, there must first be the desire to become holy. We must cleanse ourselves from all pollutions of flesh and spirit by confessing them—giving them up to God—and having them cleansed away in the blood. Then, holiness can be perfected.[8] Then, in belief of the truth that Christ Himself is our sanctification, we have to take and receive from Him what is prepared in His fullness for us.[9] We must be deeply convinced that Christ is wholly and alone our sanctification as He is our justification. We must believe that He will actually and powerfully work in us what is pleasing to God. In this faith, we must know that we have sufficient power for holiness, and that our work is to receive this power from Him by faith every day.[10] He gives His Spirit, the Holy Spirit, in us to communicate the holy life of Jesus to us.

Young Christian, the Trinity is three times holy.[11] And this Trinity is the God who sanctifies you. The Father sanctifies by giving Jesus to you and confirming you in Jesus. The Son sanctifies by becoming your sanctification and giving you the Spirit. The

---

[7]Rom. 1:4; 8:2,13; 1 Pet. 1:2
[8]2 Cor. 7:1
[9]John 1:14,16; 1 Cor. 2:9,10
[10]Gal. 2:21; Eph. 2:10; Phil. 2:13; 4:13
[11]Isa. 6:3; Rev. 4:8; 15:3,4

Spirit sanctifies by revealing the Son in you, preparing you as a temple for the indwelling of God, and making the Son live in you. Be holy, for God is holy.

Lord God, the Holy One of Israel, what thanks will I render to You for the gift of Your Son as my sanctification, and that I am sanctified in Him. And what thanks for the Spirit of sanctification to live in me, and transplant the holiness of Jesus into me. Lord, help me to understand this correctly, and to long for the experience of it. Amen.

Notes

1. What is the distinction between forgiveness and cleansing, and between cleansing and holiness?

2. What made the temple a sanctuary? The indwelling of God. What makes us holy? Nothing less than the indwelling of God in Christ by the Holy Spirit. Obedience and purity are the way to holiness; nothing is higher than holiness itself.

3. In Isaiah 57, verse 17, there is a description of the man who will become holy. It is he who, in poverty of spirit, acknowledges that even when he is living as a righteous man he has nothing, and he looks to God to come and dwell in Him.

4. No one is holy but the Lord. You have as much holiness as you have God in you.

5. The word "holy" is one of the most profound words in the Bible, the deepest mystery of the Godhead. Do you desire to understand something of it and to obtain part of it? Then take these two thoughts, "I am holy," "Be ye holy," and carry them in your heart as a seed of God that has life.

6. What is the connection between the perseverance of the saints and the perseverance in holiness?

Chapter 15
Righteousness

"He hath showed thee, O man, what is good; and what doth the Lord require of thee, but to do justly, and to love mercy, and to walk humbly with thy God?" Micah 6:8.

"Yield yourselves unto God, as those that are alive from the dead, and your members as instruments of righteousness unto God....Being then made free from sin, ye became servants of righteousness. Even so now yield your members servants to righteousness unto holiness" Romans 6:13,18,19.

The word of Micah teaches us that the fruit of the salvation of God is chiefly seen in three things. The new life must be characterized, in my relation to God and His will, by righteousness and doing right. It must be characterized in my relation to my neighbor, by love and benevolence. It must be characterized in relation to myself, by humility and lowliness. For the present, we will meditate on righteousness.

Scripture teaches us that no man is righteous before God, or has any righteousness that can stand before God.[1] It says that man receives the rightness or righteousness of Christ for nothing, and that by this righteousness—received in faith—he is justified before God.[2] This righteous sentence of God is

---

[1] Ps. 14:3; 143:2; Rom. 3:10,20
[2] Rom. 3:22,24; 10:3,10; 1 Cor. 1:30; 2 Cor. 5:21; Gal. 2:16; Phil. 3:9

something binding by which the life of righteousness is implanted in man, and he learns to live a righteous life.[3] Being right with God is followed by doing right. "The just shall live by faith" a righteous life (Galatians 3:11).

It is to be feared that this is not always understood. One sometimes thinks more of justification than of righteousness in life and walk. To understand the will and the thoughts of God, let us trace what the Scriptures teach us on this point. We will be convinced that the man who is clothed in a divine righteousness before God must also walk before God and man in a divine righteousness.

Consider how, in the Word, the servants of God are praised as righteous[4]—how the favor and blessing of God are pronounced on the righteous [5] —how the righteous are called to confidence, to joy.[6] See this especially in the Book of Psalms. See how often in Proverbs all blessing is pronounced upon the righteous.[7] See how everywhere men are divided into two classes—the righteous and the godless.[8] See how, in the New Testament, the Lord Jesus demands this righteousness.[9] See how Paul, who announces most of the doctrine of justification by faith alone, insists that this is the aim of justifica-

---

[3]Rom. 5:17,18; 6:13,18,19; 8:3; Tit. 1:3; 2:12; 1 John 2:29; 3:9,10

[4]Gen. 6:9; 7:1; Matt. 1:19; Luke 1:6; 2:25; 2 Pet. 2:7

[5]Ps. 1:6; 5:12; 14:5; 34:16,20; 37:17,39; 92:13; 97:11; 146:8

[6]Ps. 32:11; 33:1; 58:11; 64:10; 68:4; 97:12

[7]Prov. 10:3,6,7,11,16,20,21,24,25,28,30,31,32

[8]Eccles. 3:17; Isa. 3:10; Ezek. 3:18,20; 18:21,23; 33:12; Mal. 3:18; Matt. 5:45; 12:49; 25:46

[9]Matt. 5:6,20; 6:33

tion—to form righteous men, who do right.[10] See
how John names righteousness along with love as
the two indispensable marks of the children of
God.[11] When you put all these facts together, it must
be very evident to you that a true Christian is a man
who does righteousness in all things, even as God is
righteous.

Scripture will also teach you what this righteousness is. It is a life in accordance with the commands
of God, in all their depth and profoundness. The
righteous man does what is right in the eyes of the
Lord.[12] He does not obey the rules of human
action—he does not ask what man considers lawful.
A man who stands right with God, who walks
uprightly with God, dreads, above all things, even
the least unrighteousness. He is afraid, above all, of
being partial to himself and of doing any wrong to
his neighbor for the sake of his own advantage. In
great and little things alike, he takes the Scriptures
as his measure and line. As an ally of God, he knows
that the way of righteousness is the way of blessing
and life and joy.

Consider, further, the promises of blessing and
joy which God has for the righteous. Then live as one
who—in friendship with God, and clothed with the
righteousness of His Son through faith—has no
alternative but to do righteousness.

*O Lord, You have said, "There is no God else
beside Me: a just God and a Savior" (Isaiah 45:21).
You are my God. It is as a righteous God that You*

---

[10]Rom. 3:31; 6:13,22; 7:4,6; 8:4; 2 Cor. 9:9,10; Phil. 1:11; 1
Tim. 6:11
[11]1 John 2:4,11,29; 3:10; 5:2
[12]Ps. 119:166,168; Luke 1:6,75; 1 Thess. 2:10

*are my Savior and have redeemed me in Your Son.
As a righteous God, You make me righteous also,
and say to me that the righteous will live by faith.
Lord, let the new life in me be the life of faith, the life
of a righteous man. Amen.*

Notes

1. Observe the connection between the doing of
righteousness and sanctification in Romans
6:19,22—"Yield your members servants to righteousness unto holiness." "Having become servants
to God, ye have your fruit unto sanctification." The
doing of righteousness, righteousness in conduct
and action, is the way to holiness. Obedience is the
way to become filled with the Holy Spirit. And the
indwelling of God through the Spirit is holiness.

2. "Suffer it to be so now: for thus it becometh us
to fulfill all righteousness" (Matt. 3:15). It was when
Jesus had spoken that word that He was baptized
with the Spirit. Let us set aside every temptation not
to walk in full obedience toward God as He did, and
we too will be filled with the Spirit. "Blessed are they
which do hunger and thirst after righteousness"
(Matt. 5:6).

3. Take pains to set before yourselves the image of
a man who so walks that the name of "righteous" is
involuntarily given to him. Think of his uprightness,
his conscientious care to cause no one to suffer the
least injury, his holy fear and carefulness to trans-
gress none of the commands of the Lord—righteous
and walking blamelessly in all the commandments
and ordinances of the Lord. Then say to the Lord
that you should so live.

4. You understand now the great word, "The just

shall live by faith" (Gal. 3:11). By faith the godless man is justified and becomes a righteous man. By faith he lives as a righteous man.

Chapter 16
Love

"A new commandment I give unto you, That ye love one another; as I have loved you, that ye also love one another. By this shall all men know that ye are My disciples, if ye have love one to another" John 13:34,35.

"Love worketh no ill to his neighbor: therefore love is the fulfilling of the law" Romans 13:10.

"Beloved, if God so loved us, we ought also to love one another. If we love one another, God dwelleth in us, and His love is perfected in us" 1 John 4:11,12.

In the word of Micah, in the previous section, righteousness is the first thing which God demands. To love mercy is the second. Righteousness stood more in the foreground in the Old Testament. Love is first seen as supreme in the New Testament. Passages to this effect are not difficult to find. In the advent of Jesus, the love of God is first revealed, the new, eternal life is first given, and we become children of the Father and kindred to each other. On this ground the Lord can then, for the first time, speak of the New Commandment—the commandment of brotherly love. Righteousness is not required less in the New Testament than in the Old.[1] Yet the burden of the New Testament is that we have been given a power for love which was unattainable in the early days.[2]

---

[1]Matt. 5:6,17,20; 6:33
[2]Rom. 5:5; Gal. 5:22; 1 Thess. 4:9; 1 John 4:11; John 13:34

Let every Christian take it deeply to heart that in the first and the great commandment—the new commandment given by Jesus at His departure—the unique characteristic of a disciple of Jesus is brotherly love. And let him, with his whole heart, yield himself to Him to obey that command. For the right exercise of this brotherly love, one must pay attention to more than one thing.

Love of the brethren arises from the love of the Father. By the Holy Spirit, the love of God is shed abroad in our hearts, and the wonderful love of the Father is unveiled to us, so that His love becomes the life and the joy of our soul. Our love of God springs out of the fountain of His love for us.[3] And our love of Him naturally causes us to love the brethren.[4] Do not attempt to fulfill the commandment of brotherly love by yourselves—you are not in a position to do this. But believe that the Holy Spirit, who is in you to make known the love of God to you, also certainly enables you to yield this love. Never say, "I feel no love. I do not feel as if I can forgive this man." Your decision to act should not be based on feelings. Rather, it is your duty to believe the command and to have faith in God to give you the power with which to obey the command. In obedience to the Father—with the choice of your will, and in faith that the Holy Spirit gives you power—begin to say, "I *will* love him. I *do* love him." The feeling will follow the faith. Grace gives power for all that the Father asks of you.[5]

---

[3] Rom. 5:5; 1 John 4:19

[4] Eph. 4:2,6; 5:1,2; 1 John 3:1; 4:7,20; 5:1

[5] Matt. 5:44,45; Gal. 2:20; 1 Thess. 3:12,13; 5:24; Phil. 4:13; 1 Pet. 1:22

Brotherly love has its measure and rule in the love of Jesus. "This is My commandment, that ye love one another, as I have loved you."[6] The eternal life that works in us is the life of Jesus. It knows no other law than what we see in Him. It works with power in us what it worked in Him. Jesus Himself lives in us, and loves in and through us. We must believe in the power of this love in us, and, in that faith, love as He loved. Do believe that this is true salvation—to love even as Jesus loves.

Brotherly love must be in deed and in truth.[7] It is not mere feeling. The power in Christ arises from faith which works by love. It manifests itself in all the Christ-like characteristics that are specified in the Word of God. Contemplate its glorious image in 1 Corinthians 13:4-7. Notice all the glorious encouragements to gentleness, to longsuffering, to mercy.[8] In all your conduct, let it be seen that the love of Christ lives in you. Let your love be a helpful, self-sacrificing love—like that of Jesus. Hold all children of God, however sinful or wrong they may be, fervently dear. Let your love for them teach you to love all men.[9] Show your family, the Church, and the world that within you "love is greatest" (1 Corinthians 13:13). Show all that the love of God has a full dwelling and a free working in your life.

Christian, God is love. Jesus is the gift of this love—to bring love to you, to transplant you into that life of godlike love. Live in that faith, and you

---

[6]Luke 22:26,27; John 13:14,15,34; Col. 2:13

[7]Matt. 12:50; 25:40; Rom. 13:10; 1 Cor. 7:19; Gal. 5:6; Jas. 2:15,16; 1 John 3:16,17,18

[8]Gal. 5:22; Eph. 4:2,32; Phil. 2:2,3; Col. 3:12; 2 Thess. 1:3

[9]Luke 6:32,35; 1 Pet. 1:22; 2 Pet. 1:7

will not complain that you have no power to love. The love of the Spirit will be your power and your life.

Beloved Savior, I discern more clearly that the whole of the new life is a life in love. You are the Son of God's love—the gift of His love—who has come to introduce us into His love, and give us a dwelling there. And the Holy Spirit is given to shed abroad the love of God in our hearts, to open a spring out of which love will stream to You and to the believers and to all mankind. Lord, here am I, one redeemed by love, to live for it and, in its might, to love all. Amen.

Notes

1. Those who reject the Word of God sometimes say that is is of no importance what we believe if we but have love, and so they are for making love the one condition of salvation. In their zeal against this view, the orthodox party have sometimes presented faith in justification, as if love were not of so much importance. This is likely to be very dangerous. God is love. His Son is the gift, the bringer, of His love to us. The Spirit sheds the love of God in the heart. The *new life* is a life in love. Love is the greatest thing. Let it be the chief element in our life—true love which is known in the keeping of God's commandments (see 1 John 3:10,23,24; 5:2).

2. Do not wonder why I have said that you must love even though you do not feel the least bit of love. Not the feeling, but the will, is your power. It is not in your feeling, but in your faith, that the Spirit in you is the power of your will to work in you all that the Father bids you. Therefore, although you feel

absolutely no love for your enemy, say in the obedience of faith, "Father, I love him; in faith in the hidden working of the Spirit in my heart, I do love him."

3. Do not think that this is love, if you wish no evil to anyone, or if you should be willing to help, if he were in need. No, love is much more. Love is *His love*. Love is the disposition with which God addressed you when you were His enemy, and afterward ran to you with tender longing to caress you.

Chapter 17
Humility

"And what doth the Lord require of thee, but to do justly, and to love mercy, and to walk humbly with thy God?" Micah 6:8

"Learn of me that I am meek and lowly in heart: and ye shall find rest unto your souls" Matthew 11:29.

One of the most dangerous enemies the young Christian must guard against is pride or self-exaltation. There is no sin that works more cunningly and more hiddenly. It knows how to penetrate into everything, into our service for God, our prayers, and even into our humility. Self-exaltation can extract the nutrients out of even the smallest thing in earthly life and the holiest thing in spiritual life.[1] The Christian must therefore be on his guard against it. He must listen to what the Scriptures teach about it and about the humility by which it is driven out.

Man was created to have part in the glory of God. He obtains this by surrendering himself to the glorification of God. The more he seeks the glory of God to be his only trait, the more of this glory he will know for himself.[2] The more he forgets and loses himself—desiring to be nothing so that God may be

---

[1] 2 Chron. 26:5,16; 32:26,31; Isa. 65:5; Jer. 7:14; 2 Cor. 12:7
[2] Isa. 43:7,21; John 12:28; 13:31,32; 17:1,4,5; 1 Cor. 10:31; 2 Thess. 1:11,12

all and be alone glorified—the happier he will be.

Because of sin this design has been thwarted. Man seeks himself and his own will.[3] Grace has come to restore what sin has corrupted. Grace will bring man to glory if he will deny himself and live solely for the glory of God. Jesus is the example of this humility or lowliness. He gave no thought to Himself—He gave Himself over wholly to glorify the Father.[4]

He who wants to be freed from self-exaltation must not consider obtaining it by striving against its mere workings. No, pride must be driven out and kept out by humility. The Spirit of life in Christ, the Spirit of His lowliness, will work in us true humility.[5]

He will most often use the Word to bring about this sense of humility. We understand that it is by the Word that we are cleansed from sin. It is by the Word that we are sanctified and filled with the love of God.

Now observe what the Word says about this point. It speaks of God's dislike of pride and the punishment that comes with it.[6] It gives the most glorious promises to the meek.[7] In almost every Epistle, humility is commended to Christians as one of the first virtues.[8] The most important characteristic which Jesus seeks to impress upon His disciples is humility. His whole incarnation and redemption

---

[3] Rom. 1:21,23
[4] John 8:50; Phil. 2:7
[5] Rom. 8:2; Phil. 2:5
[6] Ps. 31:23; Prov. 16:5; Matt. 23:12; Luke 1:51; Jas. 4:6; 1 Pet. 5:5
[7] Ps. 34:19; Prov. 11:2; Isa. 57:15; Luke 9:48; 14:11; 18:14
[8] Rom. 12:3,16; 1 Cor. 13:4; Gal. 5:22,23,26; Eph. 4:2; Phil. 2:3

have their roots in His humiliation.[9]

Take singly some of these words of God from time to time and lay them up in your heart. The tree of life yields many different kinds of seed—among them, the seed of the heavenly plant called humility. The seeds are the words of God. Carry them in your heart. They will shoot up and bear fruit.[10]

Consider, moreover, how lovely, how becoming, how well-pleasing humility is to God. As man, created for the honor of God, you find it suitable to you.[11] As a sinner, deeply unworthy, you have nothing more to urge against it.[12] As a redeemed soul, who knows that only through the death of the natural "I" does the way to the new life lie, you find it indispensable.[13] As a child of the Father, overwhelmed with His love, you must consider it above all else.[14]

But here, as everywhere in the life of grace, let faith be the chief thing. Believe in the power of the eternal life which works in you. Believe in the power of Jesus, who is your life. Believe in the power of the Holy Spirit, who lives in you. Do not attempt to hide your pride, or to forget it, or to root it out yourself. Confess this sin—and all its workings that you can find—in the sure confidence that the blood cleanses and that the Spirit sanctifies. Learn that Jesus is meek and lowly in heart. Consider that He is your life, with all that He has. Believe that He gives His humility to you. Be clothed with humility, so that

[9]Matt.20:26,28; Luke 22:27; John 13:14,15; Phil. 2:7,8
[10]1 Thess. 2:13; Heb. 4:12; Jas. 1:21
[11]Gen. 1:27; 1 Cor. 11:7
[12]Job 42:6; Isa. 6:5; Luke 5:8
[13]Rom. 7:18; 1 Cor. 15:9,10; Gal. 2:20
[14]Gen. 32:10; 2 Sam. 7:18; 1 Pet. 5:6-10

you may be clothed with Jesus. It is Christ in you that will fill you with humility.

Blessed Lord Jesus, there never was anyone among the children of men so high, so holy, so glorious as You. And never was there anyone who was so humble and ready to deny Himself as the servant of all. Lord, when will we learn that humility is the grace by which man can be most closely conformed to the divine glory? Teach me this. Amen.

Notes

1. Take heed that you do nothing to encourage pride on the part of others. Take heed that you do not allow others to feed your pride. Take heed, above all, that you do nothing yourself to feed your pride. Let God alone, always and in all things, obtain the honor. Endeavor to observe all that is good in His children, and to thank Him heartily for it. Thank Him for all that helps you to hold yourself in small esteem, whether it is sent through friend or foe. Resolve, especially, not to be eagerly bent on your own honor when this is not accorded to you as it ought to be. Commit this to the Father. Take heed only to His honor.

2. By no means suppose that faint-heartedness or doubting is humility. Deep humility and strong faith go together. The centurion who said, "I am not worthy that Thou shouldest come under my roof," and the woman who said, "Yea, Lord, yet even the dogs eat of the crumbs," these two were the most humble and the most trustful that the Lord found (see Matt. 8:10; 15:28). The reason is this—the nearer we are to God, the less we are in ourselves, but the stronger we are in Him. The more I see of God,

the less I become, the deeper is my confidence in
Him. To become humble, let God fill eye and heart.
Where God is all, there is no time or place for man.

Chapter 18
Stumblings

"In many things we all stumble" James 3:2.

This word of God by James is the description of what man is—even the Christian—when he is not kept by grace. It serves to take away from us all hope in ourselves.[1] "Now unto Him that is able to guard you from stumbling...be glory, majesty, dominion, and power...for evermore" (Jude 24,25). This word of God by Jude points to Him who keeps us from falling, and who stirs our soul to give Him the honor and the power. It serves to confirm our hope in God.[2] "Brethren, give the more diligence to make your calling and election sure: for if ye do these things, ye shall never stumble" (2 Peter 1:10). This word of God by Peter teaches us the way in which we can become recipients of the care of the Almighty, and it confirms our having been chosen by God to walk as He did (see verses 4,8,11). It serves to lead us into diligence and conscientious watchfulness.[3]

For the young Christian, what he should think about his stumblings is often a difficult question. On this point, he should especially be on his guard against two errors. Some become discouraged when they stumble—they think that their surrender was not sincere, and they lose their confidence toward

---

[1]Rom. 7:14,23; Gal. 6:1
[2]2 Cor. 1:9; 1 Thess. 5:24; 2 Thess. 2:16,17; 3:3
[3]Matt. 26:41; Luke 12:35; 1 Pet. 1:13; 5:8-10

God.[4] Others again take it too lightly. They think
that it cannot be any other way. They seldom con-
cern themselves with stumblings and, therefore, continue to live in them.[5] Let us take these words of God
to teach us what we should think of our stumblings.
There are three lessons.

Do not let stumblings discourage you. You are
called to perfection—yet this does not come at once.
Time and patience are needed for it. Therefore,
James says, "Let patience have its perfect work that
ye may be perfect and entire."[6] Do not think that
your surrender was insincere—acknowledge only
how weak you still are. Do not think that you must
continue to stumble—acknowledge only how strong
your Savior is.

*Let stumbling arouse you to faith in the mighty
Keeper.* It is because you have not relied on Him
with a sufficient faith that you have stumbled.[7] Let
stumbling drive you to Him. The first thing that you
must do with a stumbling is to go with it to your
Jesus. Tell it to Him.[8] Confess it, and receive forgiveness. Confess it, and commit yourself with your
weakness to Him, and depend on Him to keep you.
Continually sing the song, "To Him that is mighty to
keep you, be the glory."

And then, *let stumbling make you very wise.*[9] By

---

[4]Heb. 3:6,14; 10:35

[5]Rom. 6:1; Gal. 2:18; 3:3

[6]Matt. 5:48; 2 Tim. 3:17; Heb. 13:20,21; Jas. 1:4; 1 Pet. 5:10

*The Dutch version has it: "Let endurance have a perfect work,
that ye may be perfect and wholly sincere"—Tr.

[7]Matt. 14:31; 17:20

[8]Ps. 38:18; 69:6; 1 John 1:9; 2:1

[9]Prov. 28:14; Phil. 2:12; 1 Pet. 1:17,18

faith you will strive and overcome. In the power of your Keeper, and in the joy and security of His help, you will have courage to watch. The firmer you make your commitment, the stronger the certainty that He has chosen you—He will not let you go. You will become more conscientious to live in all things only for Him, in Him, through Him.[10] By doing this, the Word of God says, you will never stumble.

Lord Jesus, as a sinner who is capable of stumbling, I give honor to You every moment. You are mighty to keep men from stumbling. Yours is the might and the power—I take You as my Keeper. I look to Your love which has chosen me and wait for the fulfillment of Your word, "Ye shall never stumble."Amen.

Notes

1. Let your thoughts about what the grace of God can do for you be taken only from the Word of God. Our natural expectations—that we must always be stumbling—are wrong. They are strengthened by more than one thing. There is secret unwillingness to surrender everything. There is the example of so many sluggish Christians. There is the unbelief that cannot quite understand that God will really keep us. There is the experience of so many disappointments when we have striven in our own power.

2. Let no stumbling be tolerated just because it seems to be a small or insignificant thing.

---

[10] 2 Chron. 20:15; Ps. 18:30,37; 44:5,9; John 5:4,5; Rom. 11:20; 2 Cor. 1:24; Phil. 2:13

Chapter 19
Jesus The Keeper

*"The Lord is thy keeper:...The Lord shall pre-
serve thee from all evil;...He shall preserve thy soul"*
Psalm 121:5,7.

*"I know Him whom I have believed, and am
persuaded that He is able to keep that which I have
committed unto Him against that day"* 2 Timothy
1:12.

The Lord has not only received you, but He will
also keep you.[1] For young disciples of Christ who
are still weak, there is no lesson that is more necessary than this. The lovely name, "the Lord thy
keeper," must be carried in the heart until the assurance of an Almighty keeping becomes as strong with
us as it was with Paul, when he spoke that glorious
word, "I know Him in whom I have believed, and I
am persuaded that He is able to guard that which I
have committed unto Him against that day." Come
and learn this lesson from him.

Learn from Paul *to deposit your pledge with
Jesus.* Paul had surrendered himself, body and soul,
to the Lord Jesus—that was his pledge which he had
deposited with the Lord. You have also surrendered
yourselves to the Lord, but perhaps not with the
clear understanding that it is in order to be *kept*
every day. Do this now daily. Deposit your soul with
Jesus as a dear pledge that He will keep it secure. Do

---

[1]Gen. 28:15; Deut. 7:9; 32:10; Ps. 17:8; 89:33,34; Rom. 11:2,29

this same thing with every part of your life. Is there something that you cannot properly hold? Your heart, because it is too worldly?[2] Your tongue, because it is too idle?[3] Your temper, because it is too passionate?[4] Your calling to confess the Lord, because you are too weak?[5] Learn, then, to deposit it as a pledge to be kept with Jesus, so that He may fulfill in you the promise of God concerning it. You often pray and strive against a sin in vain. It is because—although this too is done with God's help—*you* want to be the person who overcomes. No, entrust the matter wholly to Jesus, "the battle is not yours, but God's."[6] Leave it in His hands. Believe in Him to do it for you. "This is the victory that overcometh the world, even your faith."[7] But you must first place it wholly out of your hands and into His.

Learn from Paul to set your confidence *only on the power of Jesus*. I am persuaded that *He is able* to keep my pledge. You have an Almighty Jesus to keep you. Faith keeps itself occupied only with His omnipotence.[8] Let your faith be especially strengthened in what God is able to do for you.[9] Expect, with certainty, that He will do great and glorious things for you, entirely above your own strength. See in the Holy Scriptures how constantly the power of God

---

[2] Ps. 51:17; Jer. 31:33

[3] Ps. 31:6; 141:3

[4] Ps. 119:165; Jer. 26:3,4; John 14:27; Phil. 4:6,7; 2 Thess. 3:16

[5] Isa. 1:7; Jer. 1:9; Matt. 10:19,20

[6] Ex. 14:14; Deut. 3:22; 20:4; 2 Chron. 20:15

[7] Matt. 9:28; 1 John 5:3,4

[8] Gen. 17:1; 18:14; Jer. 32:17,27; Matt. 8:27; 28:18; Luke 1:37,49; 18:27; Rom. 4:21; Heb. 11:19

[9] Rom. 4:21; 14:4; 2 Cor. 9:8; 2 Tim. 1:13

was the foundation for the trust of His people. Take these words and hide them in your heart. Let the power of Jesus fill your soul. Ask only, "What is my Jesus able to do?" What you really trust Him with, He is able to keep.[10]

And learn also from Paul where he obtained the assurance that this power would keep his pledge. He found it *in his knowledge of Jesus.* "I know Him whom I have believed," therefore I am assured.[11] You can trust the power of Jesus, if you *know* that He is yours, if you converse with Him as your friend. Then you can say, "I know whom I have believed. I know that He holds me very dear. I know and am assured that He is able to keep my pledge." This is the sure way to the full assurance of faith. Deposit your pledge with Jesus, and give yourselves wholly into His hands. Think much on His might, and rely upon Him. Live with Him so that you may always know in whom you have believed.

Young disciples of Christ, please receive this word, "The Lord is thy keeper." For every weakness, every temptation, learn to deposit your soul with Him as a pledge. You can depend on it, you can shout joyfully over it. "The Lord shall keep you from all evil."[12]

Holy Jesus, I take You as my Keeper. Let Your name, "The Lord thy keeper," sound as a song in my heart the whole day. Teach me to deposit my case as a pledge with You in every need, and to be assured that You are able to keep it. Amen.

---

[10]John 13:1; 1 Cor. 1:8,9
[11]John 10:14,28; Gal. 2:20; 2 Tim. 4:18; 1 John 2:13,14
[12]Josh. 1:9; Ps. 23:4; Rom. 8:35

Notes

1. There was once a woman who for years, and with much prayer, had striven against her temper but could not obtain the victory. On a certain day she resolved not to come out of her room until by earnest prayer she had the power to overcome. She went out in the opinion that she would succeed. Scarcely had she been in the household when something gave her offense and caused her to be angry. She was deeply ashamed, burst into tears and hastened back to her room. A daughter, who understood the way of faith better than she, went to her and said, "Mother, I have observed your conflict. May I tell you what I think the hindrance is?" "Yes, my child." "Mother, you struggle against temper and pray that the Lord may *help* you to overcome. This is wrong. The Lord must do it alone. You must give your temper wholly into His hands. Then He takes it wholly and He keeps you." The mother could not understand this at first, but later it was made clear to her. And she enjoyed the blessedness of the life in which Jesus keeps us, and we by faith have the victory. Do you understand this?

2. The expression, "The Lord must help me to overcome," is altogether outside of the New Testament. The grace of God in the soul does not become a help to us. He will do *everything*. "The Spirit of life in Christ Jesus hath made me free from the law of sin" (Rom. 8:2).

3. When you surrender anything to the Lord for keeping, take heed to two things:
   —that you give it wholly into His hands,

—that you keep it there.

Let Him have it wholly. He will carry out your case gloriously!

Chapter 20
Power And Weakness

"He said unto me, My strength is made perfect in weakness. Therefore will I rather glory in my weakness, that the power of Christ may rest upon me. Therefore I take pleasure in weakness: for when I am weak, then am I strong" 2 Corinthians 12:9,10.

There is almost no word that is so imperfectly understood in the Christian life as the word *weakness*. Sin and shortcoming, sluggishness and disobedience, are given as the reasons for our weakness. With this interpretation of weakness, the true feeling of guilt and the sincere endeavor after progress are impossible. How can I be guilty, when I do not do what it is not in my power to do? The Father cannot demand of His child what He can certainly do independently. That, indeed, was done by the law under the Old Covenant, but the Father, under the New Covenant, does not do that. He requires nothing more of us than what He has prepared for us to do in His Holy Spirit. The new life is a life in the power of Christ through the Spirit.

The error of this mode of thinking is that people estimate their weakness, not too highly, but too meagerly. They would still do something by the exercise of all their powers, and with the help of God. They do not know that they must be nothing before God.[1] You think that you have still a little

---

[1] Rom. 4:4,5; 11:6; 1 Cor. 1:27,28

strength, and that the Father must help you by adding something of His own power to your feeble energy. This thought is wrong. Your weakness appears in the fact that you *can do nothing*. It is better to speak of utter inability, for that is what the Scriptures mean by the word "weakness." "Without me ye can do nothing." "In us is no power."[2]

Whenever the young Christian acknowledges and admits to his weakness, then he learns to understand the secret of the power of Jesus. He then sees that he is not to wait and pray to become stronger, to feel stronger. No, in his inability, he is to have the power of Jesus. By faith he is to receive it. He is to believe that it is for him, and that Jesus Himself will work in and by him.[3] It then becomes clear to him what the Lord means when He says, "My power is made perfect in your weakness." He knows to return the answer, "When I am weak, then am I—yes, then am I—strong." Yes, the weaker I am, the stronger I become. And he learns to sing with Paul, "I shall glory in my weaknesses." "I take pleasure in weaknesses." "We rejoice when we are weak."[4]

It is wonderful how glorious that life of faith becomes for him who is content to have nothing. How glorious to feel nothing in himself and to always live on the power of his Lord. He learns to understand what a joyful thing it is to know God as his strength. "The Lord is my strength and song"[5] He lives in what the Psalms so often express, "I love Thee, O Lord, my strength." "I will sing of Thy

---

[2] Chron. 16:9; 20:12; John 5:19; 15:5; 2 Cor. 1:9
[3] John 15:5; 1 Cor. 1:24; 15:10; Eph. 9:18,19; Col. 1:11
[4] 2 Cor. 11:30; 12:9,11; 13:4,9
[5] Ps. 89:13; 118:14

strength: unto Thee, O my strength, will I sing praises."[6] He understands what is meant when a psalm says, "Give strength to the Lord: the Lord will give strength to His people," and when another says, "Give strength to God: the God of Israel, He giveth strength and power to His people."[7] When we give or attribute all the power to God, then He gives it to us again.

"I have written unto you, young men, because ye are strong, and the word of God abideth in you, and ye have overcome the wicked one" (1 John 2:14). The Christian is strong in his Lord.[8] Not sometimes strong and sometimes weak, but always weak, and therefore always strong. He has merely to know and use his strength trustfully. To be strong is a command, a mandate that must be obeyed. From obedience there comes more strength. "Be of good courage and He shall strengthen thine heart" (Psalm 31:24). In faith, the Christian must simply obey the command, "Be strong in the Lord, and in the power of His might."[9]

O God of the Lord Jesus, the Father of glory, give unto us the Spirit of wisdom and of revelation in the knowledge of Jesus, so that we may know the exceeding greatness of His power toward us who believe. Amen.

Notes

1. As long as the Christian thinks of the service of God or of sanctification as something that is hard

[6]Ps. 18:1; 28:7,8; 31:4; 43:2; 46:1; 59:17; 62:7; 87:2

[7]Ps. 29:1,11; 68:35

[8]Ps. 71:16

[9]Ps. 27:14; Isa. 40:31; Eph. 6:10

and difficult, he will make no progress. He must see that this very thing is *impossible* for him. Then he will cease endeavoring to do something. He will surrender himself so that Christ may work all in him.

2. The complaint about weakness is often nothing else except an apology for our idleness. There is power to be obtained in Christ for those who will take the energy to have it.

3. "Be strong in the Lord and the power of His might" (Eph. 6:10). Mind that. I must abide in the Lord and in the power of His might, then I become strong. To have His power I must have Himself. The strength is His, and continues to be His. The weakness continues to be mine. He, the strong, works in me, the weak. I, the weak, abide by faith in Him, the strong, so that I, in the same moment, know myself to be weak and strong.

4. Strength is for work. He who wants to be strong simply to be pious will not be so. He who, in his weakness, begins to work for the Lord, will become strong.

Chapter 21
The Life Of Feeling

"We walk by faith, not by sight" 2 Corinthians 5:7.

"Blessed are they that have not seen, and yet have believed" John 20:29.

"Said I not unto thee, that, if thou wouldest believe, thou shouldest see the glory of God" John 11:40.

In connection with your conversion, there was no greater hindrance than your feelings. You thought, perhaps for years, that you must experience something, must feel and perceive something in yourselves. It seemed to you as if it were too hazardous to simply, and without some feeling, believe in the Word, and to be sure that God had received you— that your sins were forgiven. But finally you had to acknowledge that the way of faith, without feeling, was the way of the Word of God. And it has been the way to salvation for you. Through faith alone you have been saved, and your soul has found rest and peace.[1]

In the further life of the Christian, there is no temptation that is more persistent and more dangerous than this same feeling. We do not find the word "feeling" in Scripture. What we call "feeling" the Scripture calls "seeing." And it tells us without ceasing that not seeing yet still believing—believing in opposition to what we see—gives salvation. "(Abra-

---

[1]John 3:36; Rom. 3:28; 4:5,16; 5:1

ham), not being weak in faith, considered not his
own body" (Romans 4:19). Faith simply adheres to
what God says. Those who see, yet have no faith, will
not partake of the glory of God. Those who have
faith in God, but do not see, will witness His glory.[2]
The man who seeks for feeling and mourns about it
will not find it. The man who does not care for
feeling will have it overflowing. "He that findeth his
life shall lose it, and he that loseth his life for my sake
shall find it" (Matthew 10:39). Faith in the Word
later on becomes sealed with true feeling by the Holy
Spirit.[3]

Child of God, learn to live by faith. Let it be firmly
implanted in you that faith is God's way to a blessed
life. When there is no feeling of liveliness in prayer,
when you feel cold and dull in the inner chamber,
live by faith. Let your faith look upon Jesus as near
and upon His power and faithfulness. Though you
have nothing to bring to Him, believe that He will
give you all. Feeling always seeks something in itself.
Faith keeps itself occupied with what Jesus is.[4]
When you read the Word and have no feeling of
interest or blessing, read it yet again in faith. The
Word will work and bring blessing, "the word effec-
tually worketh in those that believe" (1 Thessalonians 2:13). When you feel no love, believe in the love
of Jesus, and say in faith that He knows that you still
love Him. When you have no feeling of gladness,
believe in the inexpressible joy that there is for you in
Jesus. Faith is blessedness and will give joy to those
who are not concerned about the self-sufficiency

---

[2] Chron. 7:2; Ps. 27:13; Isa. 7:9; Matt. 14:30,31; Luke 5:5
[3] John 12:25; Gal. 3:2,14; Eph. 1:13
[4] Rom. 4:20,21; 2 Tim. 1:12; Heb. 11:5,6; Jas. 5:15,16

which springs from joy, but about the glorification of God which springs from faith.[5] Jesus will surely fulfill His Word, "Blessed are they that have not seen, and yet have believed." "Said I not unto thee, that, if thou wouldest believe, thou shouldest see the glory of God?"

Every day the Christian has to choose between the life of feeling and the life of faith. Happy is he who, once and for all, has made the firm choice. For every morning, he renews the choice not to seek or listen for feeling, but only to walk by faith, according to the will of God. The faith that occupies itself with the Word—with what God has said—and, through the Word—with God Himself and Jesus His Son—will taste the blessedness of a life in God above. Feeling seeks and aims at itself. Faith honors God and will be honored by Him. Faith pleases God. Through faith the believer will receive from Him the witness in the heart that he is acceptable to God.

Lord God, the one, the only thing that You desire of Your children is that they should trust You, and that they should always hold conversation with You in that faith. Lord, let it be the one thing in which I seek my happiness, to honor and to please You by a faith that firmly holds You, the Invisible, and trusts You in all things. Amen.

Notes

1. There is indeed something marvelous in the new life. It is difficult to make it clear to the young Christian. The Spirit of God teaches him to understand it after he perseveres in grace. Jesus has laid the foundation of that life in the first word of the

---

[5]Rom. 15:13; Gal. 2:20; 1 Pet. 1:5,7,8

Sermon on the Mount: "Blessed are the poor in spirit, for theirs is the kingdom of heaven" (Matthew 5:3). A feeling of deep poverty and of royal riches, of utter weakness and of kingly might, exist together in the soul. To have nothing in itself, to have all in Christ—that is the secret of faith. And the true secret of faith is to bring this into exercise and, in hours of emptiness, to know that we still have all in Christ.

2. Do not forget that the faith God's Word speaks so much of does not stand in opposition to works alone, but also in opposition to feelings. Therefore, for a pure life of faith, you must cease to seek your salvation, not only in works, but also in feelings. Let faith always speak against feeling. When feeling says, "In myself I am sinful; I am dark; I am weak; I am poor; I am sad," let faith say, "In Christ I am holy; I am light; I am strong; I am rich; I am joyful."

Chapter 22
The Holy Spirit

"And because ye are sons, God hath sent forth the Spirit of His Son into our hearts, crying, Abba, Father" Galatians 4:6.

The great gift of the Father, through whom He obtained salvation and brought it near to us, is the Son. On the other hand, the great gift of the Son—whom He sends to us from the Father to apply to us an inner and effectual salvation—is the Holy Spirit.[1] As the Son reveals and glorifies the Father, so the Spirit reveals and glorifies the Son.[2] The Spirit is in us to transfer to us the life and the salvation that are prepared in Jesus—to make them wholly ours.[3] Jesus, who is in heaven, is made present in us, dwells in us, by the Spirit. We have seen that in order to partake of Jesus two things are always necessary—the knowledge of the sin that is in us, and the understanding of the redemption that is in Him. It is the Holy Spirit who continually promotes this double work in believers. He reproves and comforts. He convicts of sin and He glorifies Christ.[4]

The Spirit convicts us of sin. He is the light and the fire of God. Through Him sin is unveiled and consumed. He is "the Spirit of judgment and of burn-

[1]John 7:39; 14:16,26; Acts 1:4,5; 2:33; 1 Cor. 3:16
[2]John 15:26; 16:14,15; 1 Cor. 2:10,12; 12:3
[3]John 14:17,26; Rom. 8:2; Eph. 3:17,19
[4]John 16:9,14

ing," by whom God purifies His people.[5] There is no limit as to how deep repentance must be for the anxious soul who complains of not feeling his sin deeply enough. He must come daily just as he is.

The deepest conviction often occurs after conversion. To the young convert we simply have to say— let the Spirit who is in you always convince you of sin. He will make you hate sin, which formerly you knew only by name. He will make you know—and with shame confess—sin, which you had not seen in the hidden depths of your heart. He will point out to you sin, which you fancied was not with you, and which you had judged severely in others.[6] With repentance and self-condemnation, He will teach you to cast yourself upon grace as being entirely sinful. In this way, you will be redeemed and purified from sin.

Beloved brothers and sisters, the Holy Spirit is in you as the light and fire of God to unveil and to consume sin. The temple of God is holy, and you are this temple. Let the Holy Spirit in you have full mastery to point out and expel sin.[7] After He makes you know sin, He will, at every turn, make you know Jesus as your life and your sanctification.

And then the Spirit, who rebukes, will also comfort. He will glorify Jesus in you, and will take what is in Jesus and make it known to you. He will give you knowledge concerning the power of Jesus' blood to cleanse,[8] and the power of Jesus' indwelling

---

[5] Isa. 4:4; Zech. 12:10,11; Matt. 3:11,12

[6] Ps. 139:7,23; Isa. 10:17; Matt. 7:5; Rom. 14:4; 1 Cor. 2:10; 14:24,25

[7] Ps. 19:13; Mic. 3:8; 1 Cor. 3:17; 2 Cor. 3:17; 6:16

[8] 1 John 1:7,9

to keep.[9] He will make you see how literally, how completely, how certainly Jesus is with you every moment, so that He may do all his own Jesus-work in you. Yes, in the Holy Spirit, the living, almighty, and ever-present Jesus will be your portion. You will also know this, and have the full enjoyment of it. The Holy Spirit will teach you to bring all your sin and sinfulness to Jesus. He will teach you to know Jesus with His complete redemption from sin as your own. As the Spirit of sanctification, He will drive out sin in order that He may cause Jesus to live within you.[10]

Beloved young Christian, take time to understand and to become filled with the truth—*the Holy Spirit is in you.* Review all the assurances of God's Word that this is so.[11] Please, do not think, for even a moment, of living as a Christian without the indwelling of the Spirit. Take pains to have your heart filled with the faith that the Spirit lives in you and will do His mighty work. It is through faith that the Spirit comes and works.[12] Have a great reverence for the work of the Spirit in you. Seek Him every day to believe, to obey, to trust, and He will take and make known to you all that there is in Jesus. He will make Jesus very glorious to you and in you.

Father, I thank You for this gift which Jesus sent to me from You. I thank You that I am now the temple of Your Spirit, and that He dwells in me.

Lord, teach me to believe this with my whole heart, and to live in the world as one who knows that

---

[9]Eph. 3:17-20; 1 Pet. 1:5

[10]Rom. 1:4; 8:2,13; 1 Pet. 1:2

[11]Rom. 8:14,16; 1 Cor. 6:19; 2 Cor. 1:22; 6:16; Eph. 1:13

[12]Gal. 3:2,5,14; 5:5

the Spirit of God is in him to lead him. Teach me to think on this with deep reverence and loving awe, that God is in me. Lord, in that faith I have the power to be holy.

Holy Spirit, reveal to me all that is sin in me. Holy Spirit, reveal to me all that is Jesus in me. Amen.

Notes

1. The knowledge of the person and the work of the Holy Spirit is for us of just as much importance as the knowledge of the person and the work of Christ.

2. Concerning the Holy Spirit, we must endeavor to hold firm the truth that He is given as the fruit of the work of Jesus for us, that He is the power of the life of Jesus in us, and that through Him, Jesus Himself, with His full salvation, lives in us.

3. In order to enjoy all of this, we must be filled with the Holy Spirit. This simply means emptied of all else and full of Jesus. The way to be filled with the Spirit is to deny ourselves, take up the cross, and to follow Jesus. Or rather, this is the way in which the Spirit leads us to His fullness. No one has the power to enter fully into the death of Jesus unless he is led by the Spirit. But He takes him who desires this by the hand and brings him into it.

4. As the whole of salvation, the whole of the new life, is by faith, so is this also true of the gift and the working of the Holy Spirit. By faith—not by works, not in feeling—do I receive Him, am led by Him, and am filled with Him.

5. As clear and definite as my faith is in the work that Jesus only and alone finished for me, so clear and definite must my faith be in the work that the

Holy Spirit accomplishes in me—to work in me the willing and the performing of all that is necessary for my salvation.

Chapter 23

The Leading Of The Spirit

"As many as are led by the Spirit of God, they are the sons of God. The Spirit itself beareth witness with our spirit, that we are children of God" Romans 8:14,16.

The very same Spirit who *leads* us as children also assures us that we *are* children. Without His leading there can be no assurance of our relationship as children of God. True, full assurance of faith is enjoyed by him who surrenders himself entirely to the leading of the Spirit.

Of what does this leading consist? Mainly of this, that our whole, hidden, inner life is guided by Him so that it may be what it ought to be. We must firmly believe this. Our growth and increase, our development and progress, is not *our* work but His. We are to trust Him for this. As a tree or animal grows by the spirit of life given to it by God, so does the Christian grow by the Spirit of life in Christ Jesus.[1] We have to cherish the joyful assurance that the Spirit—whom the Father gives to us—guides our hidden life with His divine wisdom and power. He brings it where God will have it.

Then there are also special directions of this leading. "He will guide you into all the truth" (John 16:13). When we read the Word of God, we are to wait for the Spirit to make us experience the truth

---

[1]Hos. 14:6,7; Matt. 6:28; Mark 4:26,28; Luke 2:40; Rom. 8:2

and the essential power of what God says. He makes the Word living and powerful. He leads us into a life corresponding to the Word.[2]

When you pray, you can rely on His leading, "The Spirit also helpeth our infirmities" (Romans 8:26). He leads us to what we must desire. He leads us to the way in which we are to pray—trustfully, persistently, and mightily.[3]

He leads us in the way of sanctification. He leads us in the path of righteousness. He leads us into all the will of God.[4]

He will lead in our speaking and working for the Lord. Every child has need of Him to know and to do the work of the Father. Without Him, no child can please or serve the Father. The leading of the Spirit is the blessed privilege, the sure token, and the only power of a child of God.[5]

And how can you fully enjoy this leading? The first thing that is necessary for this is *faith*. You must take time, young Christian, to have your heart filled with the deep and living consciousness that the Spirit lives within you. Concerning what the Spirit is in you and for you, you are to read God's glorious declarations in the Word until you are filled with the conviction that you truly are a temple of the Spirit. Ignorance or unbelief on this point makes it impossible for the Spirit to speak in you and to lead you. Cherish an ever-abiding assurance that the Spirit of God lives in you.[6]

---

[2]John 6:63; 14:26; 1 Cor. 2:10,14; 1 Thess. 2:13
[3]Zech. 12:10; Rom. 8:27; Jude 20
[4]1 Thess. 5:23,24; 1 Pet. 1:2,15
[5]Matt. 10:20; Acts 1:8; Rom. 8:9,13; Gal. 4:6; Eph. 1:13
[6]Acts 19:2; Rom. 5:5; 1 Cor. 3:16; 2 Cor. 5:5; Gal. 3:5,14

Then the second thing that is necessary is this—
hold yourself still, so that you may hear the voice of
the Spirit, "He shall not cry, nor lift up, nor cause his
voice to be heard in the street" (Isaiah 42:2). He
whispers gently and quietly. Only the soul that sets
itself very silently toward God can perceive His voice
and guidance. When we become needlessly involved
with the world—its business, its cares, its enjoyments, its literature, its politics—the Spirit cannot
lead us. When our service for God is a bustling and
working in our own wisdom and strength, the Spirit
cannot be heard in us. The weak and the simple—
who are willing to have themselves taught in
humility—receive the leading of the Spirit. Sit down
every morning, and often in the day, to say, "Lord
Jesus, I know nothing; I will be silent. Let the Spirit
lead me."[7]

And then—*be obedient*. Listen to the inner voice,
and do what it says to you. Fill your heart every day
with the Word. When the Spirit reveals to you what
the Word says, take it upon yourself to do it. Therefore, you will become capable of further teaching.
The full blessing of the Spirit is promised to the
obedient.[8]

Young Christian, know that you are a temple of
the Spirit. Know that it is only through the daily
leading of the Spirit that you can walk as a child of
God, with the witness that you are pleasing the
Father.

*Precious Savior, imprint this lesson deeply on my
mind. The Holy Spirit is in me. His leading is every*

---

[7] 1 Chron. 19:12; Ps. 62:2,6; 131:2; Heb. 2:20; Zech. 4:6
[8] John 14:15; Acts 5:32

*day and everywhere indispensable for me. I cannot
hear His voice in the Word when I do not wait
silently upon Him. Lord, encircle me with Your holy
love; keep watch over me so that I may always walk
as a pupil of the Spirit. Amen.*

Notes

1. It is often asked, "How do I know that I will
continue standing, that I will be kept, that I will
increase?" The question dishonors the Holy Spirit—
it is the sign that you do not know Him or do not
trust Him. The question indicates that you are seeking the secret of strength for perseverance in yourself, and not in the Holy Spirit, your heavenly guide.

2. As God sees to it that every moment there is air
for me to breathe, so the Holy Spirit will increas-
ingly maintain life in the hidden depths of my soul.
He will not break off His own work.

3. From the time that we receive the Holy Spirit,
we have nothing to do but to honor His work, to
keep our hands off of it, and to trust Him and let
Him work.

4. The beginning and the end of the work of the
Spirit is to reveal Jesus to me and to cause me to
abide in Him. As soon as I become concerned with
the work of the Spirit in me, I hinder Him. He
cannot work when I am not willing to look upon
Jesus.

5. The voice of the Father, the voice of the good
Shepherd, the voice of the Holy Spirit, is very gentle.
We must learn to become deaf to other voices, to the
world and its news, to friends and their thoughts, to
our own ego and its desires. Then we will recognize

the voice of the Spirit. Let us often set ourselves silent in prayer, entirely silent, to offer up our will and our thoughts, and with our eyes upon Jesus, to keep ear and heart open for the voice of the Spirit.

Chapter 24
Grieving The Spirit

"Grieve not the Holy Spirit of God, whereby ye are sealed unto the day of redemption" Ephesians 4:30.

It is by the Holy Spirit that the child of God is sealed, separated, stamped, and marked as the possession of God. This sealing is not a dead or external action that is finished once and for all. It is a living process, which has power in the soul, and gives a firm assurance of faith, only when it is experienced through the life of the Spirit in us. Because of this, we are to take great care not to grieve the Holy Spirit. In Him alone can you have the joyful certainty and the full blessing of your childship every day.[1] It is the very same Spirit who leads us and witnesses with our spirit that we are children of God.

How can anyone grieve the Spirit? Above all, by yielding to sin. He is the Holy Spirit, given to sanctify us, and—for every sin from which the blood cleanses us—to fill us with the holy life of God, with God Himself. Sin grieves Him.[2] For this reason, the Word of God names the sins which, above all, we are to guard against. Notice the four great sins which Paul mentions in connection with our text.

The first is *lying.* There is no single sin in the Bible

---

[1] *Childship*—a word used by the author to express the relationship of a child. Childhood expresses the state of a child rather than the relationship.

[2] Isa. 53:10; Acts 7:51; Heb. 10:29

that is so brought into connection with the devil as lying. Lying is from hell, and it goes back to hell. God is the God of truth. And the Holy Spirit cannot possibly carry forward His blessed working in a man or woman who lies, who is insincere, who does injury to the truth. Young Christian, review with care what the Word of God says about lying and liars. Pray God that you may never speak anything but the literal truth. Do not grieve the Holy Spirit of God.[3]

Then there is *anger*. "Let all bitterness, and wrath, and anger, and clamour, and evil-speaking, be put away from you" (Ephesians 4:31). Along with lying, the most common sin which keeps the Christian from increasing in grace is the sin of temper—hastiness, the proneness to anger.[4] Christian, let all ill-temperedness be put away from you. This follows from the command not to grieve the Spirit. Believe that the Holy Spirit, the great power of God, is in you. Surrender yourself every day to His indwelling in faith that Jesus can keep you by Him. He will make and keep you gentle. Yes, believe in the power of the Father, the power of Jesus, and the power of the Holy Spirit to overcome temper.[5] Confess the sin. God will cleanse you from it. Do not grieve the Holy Spirit of God.

Then there is *stealing*. This is all sin against the property or possession of my neighbor, and all deception and dishonesty in trade, in which I wrong

---

[3]Ps. 5:6; Prov. 12:22; 21:28; John 8:44; Rev. 21:8,27; 22:15

[4]Matt. 5:22; 1 Cor. 1:10,11; 3:3; 13:1,3; Gal. 5:5,15,21,26; Col. 3:8,12; 1 Thess. 5:15; Jas. 3:14

[5]Matt. 11:29; 1 Cor. 6:19,20; Gal. 6:1; Eph. 2:16,17; Col. 1:8; 2 Tim. 1:12

my neighbor and seek my own advantage at his cost. Christ's law is love which works to the advantage of my neighbor as well as myself. The love of money and property—inseparable from self-seeking—is incompatible with the leading of the Holy Spirit. The Christian must be a man who is known to be honest, righteous, and who loves his neighbor as himself.[6]

Then the apostle says, "Let no corrupt communication proceed out of your mouth, but that which is good to the use of edifying, that it may minister grace unto the hearers" (Ephesians 4:29). Even the tongue of God's child belongs to his Lord. He must be known by his manner of speech. By his speaking, he can grieve or please the Spirit. The sanctified tongue is a blessing not only to his neighbor, but to the speaker himself. Foul talk, idle words, foolish jests—they grieve the Holy Spirit. They make it impossible for the Spirit to sanctify, to comfort, and to fill the heart with the love of God.[7]

Young Christian, please do not grieve the Holy Spirit of God by these or other sins. If you have committed such sins, confess them, and God will cleanse you from them. By the Holy Spirit you are sealed. If you want to walk in the stability and joy of faith, listen to the word, "Grieve not the Holy Spirit of God."

Lord God, my Father in heaven, I pray that you would cause me to understand what marvelous grace You are manifesting to me, giving me Your

---

[6]Luke 6:31; Rom. 13:10; 1 Thess. 4:6

[7]Prov. 10:19,20,21,31; 18:20; Eccles. 5:1,2; Matt. 12:36; Eph. 5:4; Jas. 3:9,10

Holy Spirit in my heart. Lord, let this faith be the argument and the power for cleansing me from every sin. Holy Jesus, sanctify me, that in my thinking, speaking, acting—in all things—Your image may appear. Amen.

Notes

1. The thought of the Christian about this word, "Grieve not the Holy Spirit," is a test of whether or not he understands the life of faith. For some it is a word of terror and fear. A father once brought his child to a train to go on a journey with the new governess with whom she was to remain. Before her departure he said, "I hear that she is very sensitive and takes things amiss. Take care that you do nothing to grieve her." The poor child did not have a pleasant journey. It appeared to her very grievous to be in anxious fear of one who was so prone to take everything amiss. Many have this same view of the Holy Spirit. They think that He is a Being whom it is difficult to satisfy, who thinks little of our weakness, and who, even though we take pains, is discontented when our work is not perfect.

2. Another father also brought his daughter to a train to go on a journey, and to be a time away from home, but in the company of her mother whom she loved very deeply. "You are to be a good child," said the father, "and do everything to please your mother. Otherwise you will grieve her and me." "Oh, certainly Papa!" was the joyful answer of the child. For she felt happy to be with her mother and was willing to do her utmost to be agreeable to her.

3. These are children of God to whom the Holy Spirit is so well-known in His tender, helpful love—

as the Comforter and the good Spirit—that the word, "Grieve not the Spirit of God," has for them a gentle and encouraging power. May our fear to grieve Him always be the tender, childlike fear of trustful love.

Chapter 25

Flesh And Spirit

"And I, brethren, could not speak unto you as unto spiritual, but as unto carnal, even as unto babes in Christ" 1 Corinthians 3:1.

"I am carnal, sold unto sin: to will is present with me, but to perform that which is good I find not. The law of the Spirit of life in Christ Jesus hath made me free from the law of sin and death. Ye are not in the flesh, but in the Spirit, if so be that the Spirit of God dwell in you" Romans 7:14,18; 8:2,9.

"Having begun in the Spirit, are ye now made perfect by the flesh? If ye be led by the Spirit, ye are not under the law. If we live in the Spirit, let us also walk in the Spirit" Galatians 3:3; 5:18,25.

It is of great importance for the young Christian to understand that within him there are two natures which strive against one another.[1] If we study the texts noted above, we will see that the Word of God teaches us the following truths on this point.

Sin comes from the flesh. The reason why the Christian still sins is that he yields to the flesh and does not walk by the Spirit. Every Christian has the Spirit and lives by the Spirit, but every Christian does not walk by the Spirit. If he walks by the Spirit, he will not fulfill the desires of the flesh.[2]

So long as there are strife and envy in the Chris-

---

[1]Gal. 5:17,24,25; 6:8; Eph. 4:22,24; Col. 3:9,10; 1 Pet. 4:2
[2]Rom. 8:7; 1 Cor. 3:1,3; Gal. 5:16,25

tian, the Word of God calls him carnal. He would like to do good, but he cannot. He does what he should not, because he still strives in his own strength and not in the power of the Spirit.[3]

The flesh remains under the law and seeks to obey the law. But through the flesh the law is powerless, and the endeavor to do good is vain. Its language is, "I am carnal, sold under sin: to will is present with me, but to perform that which is good is not."[4]

This is not the condition in which God would have his child remain. The Word says, "It is God which worketh in you, both to will and to do of His good pleasure" (Philippians 2:13). The Christian must not only *live* by the Spirit, but also *walk* by the Spirit. He must be a spiritual man, and live entirely under the leading of the Spirit.[5] If he walks in this way, he will no longer do what he should not. He will no longer be as in Romans 7—a newborn babe seeking to fulfill the law. But, as in Romans 8, the Spirit will set him free from the law which gives no power but brings death, and he will no longer walk in the oldness of the letter but, rather, in the newness of the Spirit.[6]

There are Christians who begin with the Spirit, but end with the flesh. They are converted, born again through the Spirit, but fall unconsciously into a life in which they endeavor to overcome sin and be holy through their own exertion—through doing their best. They ask God to help them in these endeavors and think that this is faith. They do not

[3]Rom. 7:18; 1 Cor. 3:3; Gal. 5:15,26
[4]Rom. 4:14,15; 7:4,6; 8:3,8; Gal. 5:18; 6:12,13; Heb. 7:18;
[5]Rom. 8:14; 1 Cor. 2:15; 3:1; Gal. 6:1
[6]Rom. 7:6; 8:2,13

understand what it means to say, "In me, that is, in my flesh, dwelleth no good thing" (Romans 7:18). They do not know that they are to cease from their own endeavors so that they may do God's will, wholly and only through the Spirit.[7]

Child of God, please learn what it means to say to yourself—just as you are, even after the new birth—"I am carnal, sold under sin." No longer strive to do your best under your own strength, merely asking God to help you in your endeavors. No, learn to say, "The law of the Spirit of life in Christ Jesus hath made me free from the law of sin and death." Every day, let your goal be to have the Spirit work in you. Walk by the Spirit, and you will be redeemed from the life of complaining about your inability to do good into a life of faith, in which it is God who works in you both to will and to do (Philippians 2:13).

Lord God, teach me to acknowledge with all my heart that in me, that is, in my flesh, there dwells nothing good. Teach me also to cease from every thought, as if I could with my own endeavors serve or please You. Teach me to understand that the Spirit is the Comforter, who frees me from all anxiety and fear about my own powerlessness, in order that He may work the strength of Christ in me. Amen.

Notes

1. In order to understand the conflict between flesh and Spirit, we must especially seek to have a clear insight into the connection between Romans,

---

[7]Rom. 7:18; Gal. 3:3; 4:9; 5:4,7

chapters 7 and 8. In Romans 7, verse 6, Paul spoke of the twofold way of serving God, the one in the oldness of the letter, the other in the newness of the Spirit. In Romans 7, verses 14-16, he describes the first way; in Romans 8, verses 1-16, he describes the second. This appears clearly when we observe that in chapter 7 he mentions the Spirit only once, the law more than twenty times; while in chapter 8, he mentions the Spirit sixteen times. In Romans 7 we see the regenerate soul, just as he is in himself with his new nature—desirous, but powerless to fulfill the law, and mourning as one who "is captive under the law of sin." In Romans 8 we hear him say, "the law of the Spirit of life in Christ Jesus hath has made me free from the law of sin and death." Romans 7 describes the ever-abiding condition of the Christian, contemplated as renewed, but not experiencing by faith the power of the Holy Spirit. Romans 8 describes his life in the freedom which the Spirit of God really gives from the power of sin.

2. It is important to understand that the conflict between grace and works, between faith and one's own power, between the Holy Spirit and confidence in ourselves and the flesh, always continues to go on. This applies not only to conversion and the reception of the righteousness of God, but even further into a walk in this righteousness. The Christian has to watch very carefully against the deep inclination of his heart to still work in his own behalf when he sees anything wrong in himself, or when he would follow after holiness, instead of always and only trusting in Jesus Christ, and so serving God in the Spirit.

3. In order to clarify the opposition between the

two methods of serving God, let me consecutively cite, in their entirety, the passages in which they are expressed with special distinctions. Compare them with care. Pray to God for the Spirit in order to make you understand them. Take deeply to heart the lesson as to how you are to serve God well, and how not to serve Him.

"The circumcision is that of the heart, in the Spirit, not in the letter" (Rom. 2:29).

"To him that worketh not but believeth, his faith is counted for righteousness" (Rom. 4:5).

"Ye are not under the law but under grace" (Rom. 6:14).

"We are delivered from the law, that we should serve in newness of the Spirit and not in the oldness of the letter" (Rom. 7:6).

"We know that the law is spiritual, but I am carnal, sold under sin" (Rom. 7:14).

"The righteousness of the law is fulfilled in us, who walk not after the flesh but after the Spirit" (Rom. 8:4).

"Ye have not received the Spirit of bondage again to fear, but ye have received the Spirit of adoption" (Rom. 8:15).

"The righteousness which is of the law, that the man which doeth those things shall live by them. But the righteousness which is of faith speaketh on this wise, Say not in thine heart, Who shall ascend into heaven? Who shall descend into the deep? But what saith it? The word is nigh thee, even in thy mouth, and in thy heart" (Rom. 10:5-8).

"If by grace, then it is no more of works" (Rom. 11:6).

"I live, yet not I, but Christ liveth in me" (Gal.

2:20).

"The just shall live by faith; yet the law is not of faith; but the man that doeth them shall live in them" (Gal. 3:11,12).

"If the inheritance be of the law, it is no more of promise" (Gal. 3:18).

"So that thou art no more a servant, but a son" (Gal. 4:7).

"Wherefore, brethren, we are not children of the bondwoman, but of the free" (Gal. 4:31).

"Walk in the Spirit and ye shall not fulfill the lust of the flesh" (Gal. 5:16).

"If ye be led of the Spirit, ye are not under the law" (Gal. 5:18).

"Who worship God in the Spirit and rejoice in Christ Jesus, and have no confidence in the flesh" (Phil. 3:3).

"Another priest, who is made not after the law of a carnal commandment, but after the power of an endless life" (Heb. 7:16).

4. Beloved Christian, you have received the Holy Spirit from the Lord Jesus to reveal Him and His life in you, and to mortify the working of the body of sin. Pray often to be filled with the Spirit. Live in the joyful faith that the Spirit is in you, as your Comforter and Teacher, and that through Him all will be right. Learn this text by heart, and let it live in your heart and on your lips, "We are the circumcision, which worship God in the Spirit and rejoice in Christ Jesus, and have no confidence in the flesh" (Phil. 3:3).

Chapter 26
The Life Of Faith

"The just shall live by his faith" Habakkuk 2:4.

"We are delivered from the law, that we should serve in newness of spirit, and not in the oldness of the letter" Romans 7:6.

"I live; and yet not I, but Christ liveth in me: and the life which I now live in the flesh I live by the faith of the Son of God, who loved me, and gave Himself for me" Galatians 2:20.

The word from Habakkuk is quoted three times in the New Testament as the divine representation of salvation in Christ by faith alone.[1] But that word is very often misunderstood—as if it ran, Man will be justified by faith on his conversion. The word includes this, but signifies much more. It says that the just will *live* by faith—the whole life of the righteous, from moment to moment, will be by faith.[2]

As presented in God's Word, we all know how sharp the opposition is between the grace that comes by *faith* and the law that demands our *works*. This is generally noted with reference to justification. But that distinction holds just as much for the whole life of sanctification. The just will live by faith alone. That is, they will have power to live according to the will of God. At his conversion, the sinner found it necessary to understand that there was nothing good

---

[1] Rom. 1:17; Gal. 3:11; Heb. 10:38

[2] Rom. 5:17,21; 6:11; 8:2; Gal. 2:20; 1 John 5:11,12

in him—that he must receive grace as one who was powerless and godless. As a believer, he must understand just as clearly that in him there is nothing good—that every moment he must receive his power for good from above.[3] And his work must therefore be to look up and believe and receive his power from above—from his Lord in heaven—every morning and every hour. *I am not to do what I can, and hope in the Lord to supply strength.* No, as one who has been dead—literally able for nothing in himself, and whose life is in his Lord above—I am to lean by faith on Him who will work mightily in me.[4]

Happy is the Christian who understands that his greatest danger is to fall under the law—to be eager to serve God in the flesh with his own strength. Happy is he when he realizes that he is not under the law—which demands and yet is powerless through the flesh—but is under grace where he simply has to receive what has been given. Happy is he when he fully accepts for himself the promise of the Spirit who transfers all that is in Christ to him. Yes, happy is he when he understands what it is to live by faith—to serve, not in the oldness of the letter, but in the newness of the Spirit.[5]

Let us make the words of Paul our own. They present the true life of faith to us, "I am crucified with Christ; nevertheless I live" (Galatians 2:20). Not only my sin, but my flesh, all that is of myself— my own living and willing, my own power and working—I have given up to death. I no longer live

---

[3] Rom. 7:18; 8:2,13; Heb. 11:33

[4] Rom. 4:17; 2 Cor. 1:9; Col. 1:29; 2:3

[5] Rom. 7:4,6; 12:5,6; Gal. 5:18; Phil 3:3

of myself. I cannot. I will not live or do anything.[6] Christ lives in me. He Himself—by His Spirit—is my power, and teaches and strengthens me to live as I ought to. And that life which I now live in the flesh, I live by faith in Him. It is my responsibility to believe in Him to work the willing as well as the accomplishment.

Young Christian, let this life of faith be your faith.

Lord Jesus, You are my life. Yes, my life. You live in me, and are willing to take my whole life into Your own hands. And my whole life may be a joyful trust and experience that You are working all in me daily.

Precious Lord, to that life of faith I will surrender myself. Yes, to You I surrender myself, to teach me and to reveal Yourself fully in me. Amen.

Notes

1. Do you understand the error in saying—if the Lord helps me? The Lord must help me. In natural things we speak like this because we have a certain measure of power, and the Lord will increase it. But the New Testament never uses the word "help" of the grace of God in the soul. We have absolutely no power—God is not to help us, because we are weak. No, He is to give His life and His power in us because we are entirely powerless. He who discerns this correctly will learn to live by faith alone.

2. "Without faith it is impossible to please God; Whatsoever is not of faith is sin" (Rom. 14:23). Such words of the Spirit of God teach us how every deed and disposition of our life is to be full of faith.

3. Hence, our first work every day is to exercise

---

[6]John 15:4,5; 1 Cor. 15:10; 2 Cor. 12:9,10

faith in Jesus as our life, to believe that He dwells in us, and will do all for us and in us. This faith must be the mood of our soul the whole day. This faith cannot be maintained except in the fellowship and nearness of Jesus Himself.

4. This faith has its power in the mutual surrender of Jesus and the believer to each other. Jesus first gives Himself wholly for us. Then, the believer gives himself wholly in order to be taken into possession and to be guided by Jesus. Then the soul cannot even doubt if He will do all for it.

Chapter 27

The Might Of Satan

"Simon, Simon, behold Satan hath desired to have you, that he might sift you as wheat: but I prayed for thee, that thy faith fail not" Luke 22:31,32.

Nothing makes an enemy more dangerous than the fact that he remains hidden or forgotten. Of the three great enemies of the Christian—the world, the flesh, and the devil—the last is the most dangerous. Not only because it is he who lends the others what power they have, but also because he is not seen and, therefore, little known or feared. The devil has the power of darkness. He darkens the eyes, so that men do not know him. He surrounds himself with darkness, so that he is not observed. Yes, he even has the power to appear as an angel of light.[1] It is by the faith that recognizes things unseen that the Christian is to endeavor to know Satan—even as the Scriptures have revealed him.

When the Lord Jesus was living on earth, His great work was to overcome Satan. When He was filled with the Spirit at His baptism, the Spirit brought Him into contact with Satan as head of the world of evil spirits, and He was to combat and overcome him.[2] After that time, the eyes of the Lord were always open to the power and working of

---

[1]Matt. 4:6; 2 Cor. 4:4; 11:14
[2]Matt. 4:1,10

127

Satan. In all sin and misery He saw the revelation of
the mighty kingdom of the evil one. He saw the
enemy of God and man, not only in the demoniacs,
but also in the sick.[3] Jesus saw the work of Satan in
Peter's advice to avoid the cross, and in his denial of
the Lord. Yet, we would have considered those
events to be the natural revelation of Peter's character.[4] In His own suffering—where we rather speak of
the sin of man and the permission of God—Jesus
perceives the power of darkness. His whole work in
living and in dying was to destroy the works of
Satan. As likewise, He will utterly destroy Satan
himself at His second coming.[5]

His word to Peter, compared with the personal
experience of the Lord, gives us a fearful insight into
the work of the enemy. "Satan hath desired to have
you," says Jesus. "As a roaring lion, he walketh
about, seeking whom he may devour," says Peter
himself later on (1 Peter 5:8).[6] He does not have
unlimited power, but he is always eager to make use
of every weak or unguarded moment. "That he
might sift you as wheat." What a picture! This
world, even the Church of Christ, is the threshing
floor of Satan. The corn belongs to God—the chaff
is Satan's own. He sifts and sifts continually, and all
that falls through with the chaff, he tries to take for
himself. And many a Christian falls through in a
terrible fashion and, were it not for the intercession

---

[3]Matt. 12:28; Mark 4:15; Luke 13:16; Acts 10:38

[4]Matt. 16:23; Luke 22:31,32

[5]Luke 10:18; 22:3,53; John 12:31; 14:30; 16:11; Rom. 16:20;
 Col. 2:15; 2 Thess. 2:8,9; 1 John 3:8

[6]1 Cor. 7:5; 2 Cor. 2:10,11

of his Lord, would perish forever.[7]

Satan has more than one sieve. The first is generally worldly-mindedness—the love of the world. Many are spiritual in time of poverty, but when they become rich, they again eagerly strive to win the world. Or in the time of conversion and awakening they appear very zealous, but through the cares of the world, they are led astray.[8]

A second sieve is self-love and self-seeking. Whenever anyone does not give himself undividedly to serve his Lord and his neighbor—to love his neighbor in the Lord—it soon appears that he lacks the principal characteristic of a disciple. It will be made clear that many who profess devotion to the service of God utterly fail on this point and must be regarded with the chaff. Lovelessness is the sure sign of the power of Satan.[9]

Still another sieve, a very dangerous one, is self-confidence. Under the name of following the Spirit, one may listen to the thoughts of his own heart. He is zealous for the Lord, but with a carnal zeal, in which the gentleness of the Lamb of God is not seen. Without being observed, the movements of the flesh mingle with the workings of the Spirit. While he boasts that he is overcoming Satan, he is being secretly ensnared by him.[10]

What a serious life here on earth, where God gives Satan permission to set his threshing floor even in the Church. Happy are they who, with deep humility, fear and trembling, distrust themselves. Our

---

[7] 1 Cor. 5:5; 1 Tim. 1:20

[8] Matt. 4:9; 13:22; 1 Tim. 6:9,10; 2 Tim. 4:10

[9] John 8:44; 1 John 3:10,15; 4:20

[10] Gal. 3:3; 5:13

only security is in the intercession and guidance of Him who overcame Satan.[11] Far be it from us to think that we know all the depths of Satan and are a match for all his cunning strategies. As well as in the visible, he works and has power in the region of the spirit—the invisible. Let us fear that while we have known and overcome him in the visible, he might prevail over us in the spiritual. May our only security be the conviction of our frailty and weakness, and our confidence in Him who certainly keeps the humble heart.

Lord Jesus, open our eyes to know our enemy and his wiles. Cause us to see him and his realm, that we may dread all that is of him. And open our eyes to see how You have overcome him, and how in You we are invincible. Teach us what it is to be in You, to mortify all that is of the mere ego and the will of the flesh, and to be strong in weakness and lowliness. And teach us to bring into prayer the conflict of faith against every stronghold of Satan, because we know that You will destroy him under our feet. Amen.

Notes

1. What comfort does the knowledge of the existence of Satan give us? We know that sin is derived from a foreign power which has thrust itself into our nature and does not naturally belong to us. We know, besides, that he has been entirely vanquished by the Lord Jesus, and thus has no power over us so long as we abide trustfully in Christ.

2. The whole of this world, with all that is in it, is under the domination of Satan. Therefore, there is

---

[11]Eph. 6:10,12,16

nothing, even what appears to be good and fair, that may not be dangerous for us. In all things, even in what is lawful and right, we must be led and sanctified by the Spirit if we want to continue to be liberated from the power of Satan.

3. Satan is an evil spirit. Only by the good Spirit, the Spirit of God, can we offer resistance to him. He works in the invisible. In order to combat him, we have to enter into the invisible by prayer. He is a mighty prince. Only in the name of One who is mightier, and in fellowship with Him, can we overcome.

4. What a glorious work is labor for souls, for the lost, for drunkards, for heathen—a battle to rescue them from the might of Satan (Acts 26:18).

5. In the book of Revelation, the victory over Satan is ascribed to the blood of the Lamb (Rev. 12:11). Christians have also testified that there is no power in temptation, because Satan readily retreats when one appeals to the blood. It is by the blood that sin has been entirely expiated, and we are thus also wholly freed from his power.

Chapter 28
The Conflict Of The Christian

"Strive to enter in by the narrow door" Luke 13:24.

"Fight the good fight of faith" 1 Timothy 6:12. *"I have fought a good fight, I have finished my course, I have kept the faith"* 2 Timothy 4:7.

These texts speak of a twofold conflict. The first is addressed to the unconverted—"Strive to enter in by the narrow door." Entrance by a door is the work of a moment. The sinner is not to strive to enter during his whole lifetime. He is to strive and do it immediately. He is not to allow anything to hold him back—he must enter in.[1]

Then comes the second, the lifelong conflict—by the narrow door I come upon the new way. On the new way there will always be enemies. Of this lifelong conflict Paul says, "I have fought a good fight, I have finished my course, I have kept the faith." With respect to the continuous conflict, he gives the charge, "Fight the good fight of faith."

There is much misunderstanding about this twofold conflict. Many strive all their life against the Lord and His summons. Because they are not at rest, but feel an inner conflict, they think that this is the conflict of a Christian. Assuredly, it is not. This is one—not willing to abandon everything and surrender himself to the Lord—who struggles against

---

[1]Gen. 19:22; John 10:9; 2 Cor. 6:2; Heb. 4:6,7

God.[2] This is not the conflict that the Lord would have. What He says is that the conflict is concerned with entering in—but not a conflict for long years. No, He desires that you should break through the enemies who hold you back, and immediately enter in.

Then follows the second conflict, which endures for life. Twice Paul calls this the fight of faith. The chief characteristic of it is faith. He who well understands that the principal element in the battle is to believe, and who acts accordingly, will certainly succeed. In another passage Paul says to the Christian combatant, "Above all, taking the shield of faith, wherewith ye shall be able to quench all the firey darts of the wicked one."[3]

And what then does it mean, this "fight of faith"? That, while I strive, I must believe that the Lord will help me? No, it is not so, although it is often misunderstood as such.

In a conflict, it is of supreme importance that I be in a stronghold or fortress which cannot be taken. With such a stronghold, a weak garrison can offer resistance to a powerful enemy. Our conflict as Christians is now no longer concerned with going into the fortress. No, we have gone in, are now in, and so long as we remain in it, we are invincible. The stronghold, this stable fort, is Christ.[4] By faith we are in Him. By faith we know that the enemy can make no progress against our fortress. All of Satan's wiles go forth on the line of enticing us out of our fortress—engaging us in conflict with him on the

[2] Acts 5:39; 1 Cor. 10:22

[3] Eph. 6:16; 1 John 5:4,5

[4] Ps. 18:2,3; 46:1,2; 62:2,3,6-8; 144:2

open plain. There he always overcomes. But if, in faith, we strive and abide in Christ, then we overcome Satan, because he has to deal with Him who fights and overcomes.[5] "This is the victory that overcometh the world, even our faith" (1 John 5:4). Our first and greatest work is thus *to believe*. As Paul said before he mentions the warlike equipment of the Christian, "My brethren, be strong in the Lord, and in the strength of His might" (Ephesians 6:10).

The reason why the victory is only by faith, and why the fight of faith is the good fight, is this—it is the Lord Jesus who purchased the victory, and who alone gives power and dominion over the enemy. If we abide in Him, surrender ourselves to live in Him, and by faith appropriate what He is, then the victory is in itself our own. Then we understand—"The battle is not yours, but God's. The Lord shall fight for you, and ye shall hold your peace" (2 Chronicles 20:15; Exodus 14:14). Except that we be in Christ, pleasing Him, opposition to Satan can achieve nothing good. In ourselves we achieve nothing, but in Christ we are more than conquerors. By faith we stand in Him, righteous before God, and likewise so in Him, we are strong against our enemies.[6]

In this light we can read and understand all the noble passages in the Old Testament—especially in the Psalms—where the glorious conflict of God in behalf of his people is spoken of. Fear or spiritlessness or uncertainty weakens and cannot overcome. Faith in the living God is equal to everything.[7] In Christ this truth is now still more real. God has come

---

[5] Josh. 5:14; John 16:33; Rom. 8:37; 2 Cor. 2:14

[6] Ps. 44:4-8; Isa. 45:24

[7] Deut. 20:3,8; Josh. 6:20; Judg. 7:3; Ps. 18:32-40; Heb. 11:23

near. His power works in us who believe—it is really He who fights for us.

Lord Jesus, who is the Prince of the army of the Lord, the Hero, the Victor, teach me to be strong in You, my stronghold, and in the power of Your might. Teach me to understand what the good fight of faith is. Teach me that the one thing I need is to always look to You, the supreme Guide of faith. And consequently, in me, too, let this be the victory that overcomes the world, namely, my faith. Amen.

Notes

1. The conflict of faith is no civil war, in which one half of the kingdom is divided against the other. This would be insurrection. This is the one conflict that many Christians know—the unrest of the conscience, and the powerless wrestling of a will which consents to that which is good, but does not perform it. The Christian does not have to overcome himself. This his Lord does when he surrenders himself. Then he is free and strong to combat and overcome the enemies of his Lord and of the Kingdom. No sooner, however, are we willing that the Lord should have His way with us than we are found striving against God. This also is truly conflict, but it is not the good fight of faith.

2. In Galatians 5, reference is made to the inner conflict because the Galatians had not yet entirely surrendered themselves to the Spirit—to walk after the Spirit. The believer must not strive against the flesh to overcome it. This he cannot do. What he is to do is to choose to whom he will subject himself. By the surrender of faith in Christ, to strive in Him through the Spirit, he has a divine power for over-

coming.

3. Hence, as we have seen in connection with the beginning of the new life, our one work every day and the whole day is to believe. Out of faith come all blessings and powers, and also the victory for overcoming.

Chapter 29

Be A Blessing

"Get thee out of thy country, and from thy kindred, and from thy father's house, unto the land that I will show thee; and I will make of thee a great nation, and I will bless thee; and thou shalt be a blessing" Genesis 12:1,2.

In these first words that God spoke to Abraham, we have the short summary of all that God has to say to him and to us as His children. We see the goal to which God calls us, the power that carries us to that goal, and the place where that power is found.

Be a blessing—that is the goal for which God separates Abraham and every believing child of His.

God would have him and us understand that, when He blesses us, it is not to simply make us happy, but so that we would still further communicate His blessing.[1] God Himself is love, and therefore He blesses. Love does not seek itself. When the love of God comes to us, it will seek others through us.[2] From the beginning, the young Christian must understand that he has received grace with the definite aim of becoming a blessing to others. Please, do not keep for yourself what the Lord gives to you for others. Offer yourself expressly and completely to the Lord—to be used by Him for others. That is the way to be blessed overflowingly yourself.[3]

---

[1] Matt. 5:44,45; 10:8; 18:33
[2] Isa. 58:10,11; 1 Cor. 13:5; 1 John 4:11

The power for this work will be given. "Be a blessing," "I will bless thee," says the Lord. You are to be personally blessed and sanctified. You are to be filled with the Spirit, peace, and power of the Lord. Then you have power to bless.[4] In Christ, God has blessed us with all spiritual blessings (Ephesians 1:3). Let Jesus fill you with these blessings, and you will certainly *be* a blessing. You do not need to doubt or fear. The blessing of God includes in it the power of life for multiplication, for expansion, for communication. See in the Scriptures how blessing and multiplication go together.[5] Blessing always includes the power to bless others. Only give the word of the Almighty God, "I will bless thee," time to sink into your spirit. Wait upon God, so that He Himself may say to you, "I will bless thee." Let your faith cleave firmly to this. God will make it truth to you, above all asking and thinking.[6]

But for this reason you must also take yourself to the place of blessing—the land of promise, and the simple life of faith in those promises. "Get thee out of thy country and thy father's house," says the Lord. God would have departure and separation from the life of nature and the flesh, in which we are born of Adam. The offering up of what is most precious to man is the way to the blessing of God.[7] "Get thee to a land that I will show thee," says the Lord, "out of the old life into a new life, where I

---

[3]Ps. 112:5,9; Prov. 11:24,25; Matt. 25:40; 1 Cor. 15:58; 2 Cor. 9:6; Heb. 6:10

[4]Luke 24:49; John 7:38; 14:12

[5]Gen. 1:22,28; 9:1; 22:17; 26:24

[6]2 Cor. 9:8,11; Heb. 6:14

[7]Luke 18:29,30; John 12:24,25; 2 Cor. 6:17,18

alone am your guide." That is, a life where God can have me wholly for Himself alone, and where I walk only on the promises of God—a life of faith.

Christian, God will in a divine fashion fulfill to you His promise, "I will bless thee." Leave your homeland, your father's house, and your life and involvement with the world and the ways of the flesh. Enter into the *new life*—the life of the Spirit, the life in fellowship with God—to which He will lead you. There you become receptive to His blessing. There your heart becomes open to full faith in His word, "I will bless thee." There He can fulfill that word to you, and make you full of His blessing and power to be a blessing to others. Live with God, separated from the world. Then you will hear the voice of God speak with power: "I will bless thee"; "Be thou a blessing."

Father, show me the way to that promised land where You bring Your people to have them wholly for Yourself. I will abandon everything to follow You, to hold converse with You alone, in order that You may fill me with Your blessing. Lord, let Your word, "I will bless thee," live in my heart as a Word of God. Then will I give myself wholly to live for others and to be a blessing. Amen.

Notes

1. God is the great, the only Fountain of blessing. As much of God as I have in me, so much blessing can I bring. I can work much for others without blessing. To actually *be* a blessing, I must begin with that word, "I will bless thee," then the other, "Be a blessing," becomes easy.

2. In order to become a blessing, begin on a small scale. Yield yourself up for others. Live to make others happy. Believe that the love of God lives in you by the Spirit, and give yourself wholly to be a blessing and a joy to those who are around you. Pray to God to shed abroad His love in you still further by the Spirit. And believe very firmly that God can make you a greater blessing than you can think if you surrender yourself to Him for this purpose.

3. But this surrender must have time in solitary prayer, so that God may obtain possession of your spirit. This is for you the departure from your father's house. Separate yourself from men so that God may speak with you.

4. What do you think? Was Abraham ever filled with regret that he placed himself so entirely under the leading of God? Then do the same.

5. Do you now know the two words which are the source of all promises and all commands to the children of believing Abraham? The promise is: "I will bless thee." The command is: "Be a blessing." Please take them both firmly for yourself.

6. And do you now understand where these two words to Abraham are fulfilled? In separation from his father's house—in the walk in fellowship with God.

Chapter 30
Personal Work

"Restore unto me the joy of Thy salvation: and uphold me with Thy free spirit. Then will I teach transgressors Thy ways; and sinners shall be converted unto Thee" Psalm 51:12,13.

"I believe, therefore have I spoken" Psalm 116:10.

"But ye shall receive power, after that the Holy Ghost is come upon you" Acts 1:8.

Every redeemed man is called to be a witness for his Lord. Not only by a godly walk, but by personal effort I should serve and make my Lord known. My tongue—my speech—is one of the principal means of communicating with and influencing others. When I do not offer up my lips to speak for the Lord, I am serving Him with only a partial dedication.[1]

There is an inconceivably great need for this work. There are thousands of Christians who continually enjoy the preaching of the Word, and yet they do not understand the way of salvation. The Lord Jesus not only preached to the multitudes, but He also spoke to individuals according to their needs.[2] Scripture is full of examples of those who told others what the Lord had done for them, and who then became a blessing themselves.[3] The teacher alone cannot do this work of personal speaking. Every redeemed soul

---

[1]Ps. 40:10,11; 66:16; 71:8,15,24; Heb. 13:15

[2]Luke 7:40; John 3:3; 4:7

[3]Ex. 18:8,11; 2 Chron. 5:13

must cooperate with him. He is in the world as a witness for his Lord. His own life cannot come to its full healthy increase, if he does not confess his Lord and work for Him.

That witness for the Lord must be a personal witness. We must have the courage to say, "He has redeemed me; He will also redeem you. Will you not accept this redemption? Come, let me show you the way."[4] There are hundreds who would be glad if the personal question were put to them, "Are you redeemed? What keeps you back? Can I help you go to the Lord?" Parents should personally speak with their children, and ask them the question, "My child, have you already received the Lord Jesus?" When teaching the Word of God, Sunday school teachers and day school teachers should ask the children if they have really received salvation. They should also seek the opportunity to individually ask each child this personal question. Friends must speak with their friends. Yes, this work should be done before all else.

Such work must be the work of love. Let others feel that you love them tenderly. Let the humility and gentleness of love, as was seen in Jesus, be also seen in you. At every turn, surrender yourself to Jesus so that you will be filled with His love. Not by feeling, but by faith in this love, can you do your work. "Beloved, keep yourselves in the love of God. And on some have compassion, and others save, pulling them out of the fire; and on some have mercy with fear" (Jude 21-23). The flesh often thinks that strength and force do more than love and patience. But that is not so. Love achieves everything—it has

---

[4]John 1:41,42,46; 4:28,29,39; Acts 11:19

overcome on the cross.[5]

Such work must be the work of faith—faith working by love. Faith that the Lord desires to use you and will use you. Do not be afraid on account of your weakness. Learn in the Scriptures what glorious promises God gave to those who had to speak for Him.[6] Surrender yourself continually to God to be used for the rescue of souls. Take your stand on the fact that He, who has redeemed you for this end, will for this end also bless you. Although your work is in weakness and fear, and although no blessing appears to come, be of good courage—at His time, we will reap.[7] Be filled with faith in the power of God, in His blessing upon you, and in the certainty that He hears prayer. "If any man see his brother sinning a sin which is not unto death, he shall ask, and God shall give him life" (1 John 5:16). Whether he that does not know sin is the most miserable and neglected, or whether he is decent but indifferent, take courage—the Lord is mighty to bless. He hears prayer.

But above all—for this is the principal point— carry out this work in fellowship with Jesus. Live closely with Him—live entirely for Him. Let Jesus be all in your own life, and He will speak and work in you.[8] Be full of the blessing of the Lord, full of His Spirit and His love, and it can be no other way than that you will be a blessing. You will be able to share what He continually is for you. You will have the lov﹖ and the courage—with all humility—to ask

---

[5]Heb. 3:13; 10:24

[6]Ex. 4:11,12; Josh. 1:9; Isa. 50:4,11; Jer. 1:6,7; Matt. 10:19,20

[7]2 Chron. 15:7; Ps. 126:6; Hag. 2:5; Gal. 6:9

[8]Acts 4:13; 2 Cor. 3:5; 13:3

souls the question, "Is it well with you? Have you indeed received the Lord Jesus as your Savior?" And the Lord will have you experience the rich blessing which is promised to those who live to bless others.

Young Christian, be a witness for Jesus. Live as one who is wholly given to Him, to watch and to work for His honor.

Blessed Lord, who has redeemed me to serve the Father in the proclamation of His love, I will, with a free spirit, offer myself to You for this end. Fill my heart with love for Him, for You, and for souls. Cause me to see what an honor it is to do the work of redeeming love, even as You did it. Strengthen my confidence that You are working with Your power in my weakness. And let my joy be to help souls to find You. Amen.

Notes

1. The question is often asked, "What can I do to work for the Lord?" Can you not teach a class in the Sunday school? Perhaps you live in the country where there are children who have no hour of the Lord's day devoted to them. Perhaps there are heathen children, or even grown-up people of the farms, who do not go to church. See whether you cannot gather them together in the name of Jesus. Make it a matter of prayer and faith. Although you do this work with trembling, you may be sure that to begin to work will make you strong. Or, can you do nothing for the circulation of books and tracts? When you have a book that has been useful to you, order six or twelve copies of it. Speak of it, and offer it to others. You can do great service by this means. So also with tracts. If you are too poor to give them

for nothing, have them to sell. You may procure blessing by this method. It will especially help you to speak to others if you begin with telling them what is in a book.

2. But the main thing is personal speaking. Do not hold back because you feel no freedom. The Lord will give you freedom in His own time. It is incredible how many are lost through ignorance. No one has ever personally made it clear to them how they can be saved. The thought that a change must first be sought and felt is so deeply rooted that the most faithful preaching is often of no avail against it. By their erroneous ideas, people misunderstand everything. Begin then to speak and to help souls to understand that they are to receive Jesus just as they are, that they can certainly know that He receives them, and that this is the power of a new and holy life.

Chapter 31
Missionary Work

"And He said unto them, Go ye into all the world, and preach the gospel to every creature. And they went forth, and preached everywhere, the Lord working with them, and confirming the word with signs following" Mark 16:15,20.

Every friend of Jesus is a friend of missions. Where there is a healthy spiritual life, there is a love for the missionary cause. When you consider the reasons for this, you obtain an insight into the glory of missions and into your calling to embrace this cause as a part of your soul's life. Come and hear how much there is to make missionary work glorious and precious.

1. It is the cause for which Jesus left the throne of heaven. The heathen are His inheritance, given to Him by His Father. The power of Satan has been established in heathendom. Jesus must have Himself vindicated as the Conqueror. His glory, the coming and manifestation of His Kingdom, depend on missions.[1]

2. Missionary work is the principal aim of the Church on earth. All the last words of the Lord Jesus teach us this.[2] The Lord is the head, and He has made himself dependent upon His body, His

---

[1] Ps. 2:3; Matt. 24:14; 28:18,19,20; Mark 13:10; Luke 21:24; Rom. 11:25

[2] Mark 16:15; Luke 24:47; John 17:18; Acts 1:8

members—by whom alone He can do His work.[3] As a member of Christ, as a member of the Church, will I not give myself to take part in the work, so that this goal may be reached?

3. It is the work for which the Holy Spirit was given. See this in the promise of the Spirit—in the leading of the Spirit—graciously given to Peter and Barnabas and Saul.[4] In the history of the Church, we find that times of revival go hand in hand with a new zeal for the missionary cause. The Holy Spirit is always a holy enthusiasm for the extension of the Kingdom.

4. Missionary work brings blessing on the Church. It enthuses heroic deeds of faith and self-denial. It has furnished the most glorious instances of the wondrous power of the Lord. It gives heavenly joy over the conversion of sinners to those who watch for it with love and prayer. It cleanses the heart to understand God's great plans, and to await the fulfillment of them in supplication. Missionary work is an example of life in a church, and brings more life.[5]

5. What a blessing it is for the world. What would we have been if missionaries had not come to our heathen forefathers in Europe? What a glorious blessing missionary work has already won in some lands. What help is there for the hundred millions of heathen, if not in missions?[6] Heaven and hell look on missions as being the battlefield where the powers of Jesus Christ and Satan encounter one another. Alas!

---

[3] 1 Cor. 12:21
[4] Acts 1:8; 11:12,23,24; 13:2,4; 22:21
[5] Acts 14:27; 15:4,5; Rom. 11:25,33; 15:10; Eph. 3:5,8,10
[6] Isa. 49:6,12,18,22; 54:1,2

that the conflict should be carried on so feebly.

6. There will be a blessing for your own soul in love for missionary work.[7]

You will have the opportunity to exercise your faith. Missionary work is a cause for faith, where everything goes on slowly, and not according to the inclinations of men. You will learn to cling to God and His Word.

Love will be awakened. You will learn to go out of yourselves and your little circle with an open eye and a large heart—to live in the interests of your Lord and King. You will realize how little true love you have, and you will receive more of that love.

You will be drawn into prayer. Your calling and power as an intercessor will become clearer to you, and you will receive the blessedness of working for the Kingdom. You will discover that the highest conformity to Him, who came to seek the lost, is the surrender of your own ease and rest to the loving fight of prayer—in behalf of the heathen—against Satan.

Young Christian, missionary work is more glorious and holy than you suppose. There is more blessing in it than you are aware of. The new life in you depends on it more than you can yet understand. Yield yourself again in obedience to the Word to give missions a large place in your heart—yes, in your heart. The Lord Himself will further teach and bless you.

And if you want to know how to increase your love for missions as the work of your Lord, devote yourself to the following guidelines. Become acquainted with the missionary cause. Read writings

---

[7]Prov. 11:24,25; Isa. 58:7,8

and books to know the condition and needs of the heathen, to know what, by the blessing of the Lord, has already been done for them, and what work is now being done. Speak with others about this cause. Perhaps a little missionary society could be instituted in your neighborhood. Perhaps one of your prayer meetings, say, once a month, could be set apart for prayer in behalf of the missionary cause. Also pray for this in private. Let the coming of the Kingdom have a definite place in your personal prayers. Strive to follow the material for prayer that is provided in the promises of God's Word—in the whole of Scripture and especially in the prophet Isaiah—in regards to the heathen.[8] Give also for missions. Not only when you are asked—not merely when you can spare without feeling it—but set apart a portion of what you possess or earn for this cause. Let the Lord see that you are earnest about His work. If there is missionary work that is being done in your neighborhood, be a friend to it. Although there may be much imperfection in that work—and where is there work of man that is perfect?—do not complain of the imperfection.

Son of God, when You did breathe Your Spirit upon Your disciples, saying, "Receive ye the Holy Ghost," You added, "As the Father hath sent Me, even so send I you." Lord, here I am—send me also. Breathe Your Spirit into me also, so that I may live for Your Kingdom. Amen.

---

[8]Isa. 49:6,18,21,22; 54:1,3; 60:1,3,11,16; 62:2

Notes

1. "Unknown makes unbeloved" is a saying that is especially true of missionary work. He who is acquainted with the wonders that God has worked in some lands will praise and thank God for what the missionary enterprise has achieved and will be strengthened in his faith that missionary work is really God's own cause. Among the books that help to awaken interest in missions are biographies of missionaries. Books on missions are generally found in church libraries (*or Christian bookstores*).

2. We should never forget that the missionary cause is an enterprise of faith. It requires faith in the promises of God, in the power of God. It has need of love—love to Jesus, by which the heart is filled with desire for His honor, and love to souls, with a heart that longs for their safety. It is a work of the Spirit of God, "whom the world cannot receive" (John 14:17). Therefore, the world can approve of missions only when they go forward with the highest prosperity.

3. Let no friend of missions become discouraged when the work proceeds slowly. Although all baptized men in the heathen nations are not truly converted, although even among the converts there is still much distortion, although some fall back after a fair profession, everything is by no means perfect among the civilized either. Among our forefathers in Europe, a whole century was required for the introduction of Christianity. Sometimes a nation received Christianity only to cast it off again after thirty or forty years. It required a thousand years to bring them up to the height at which we now stand.

Let us not expect too much from the heathen at once, but with love and patience and firm faith, pray and work and expect the blessing of God.

Chapter 32
Light And Joyfulness

"Blessed is the people that know the joyful sound: they shall walk, O Lord, in the light of Thy countenance. In Thy name shall they rejoice all the day" Psalm 89:15,16.

"Light is sown for the righteous, and gladness for the upright in heart" Psalm 97:11.

"I am the Light of the world: he that followeth Me shall not walk in darkness, but shall have the light of life" John 8:12.

"I will see you again, and your heart shall rejoice, and your joy no man taketh from you" John 16:22.

"As sorrowful, yet always rejoicing" 2 Corinthians 6:10.

A father will always be eager to see his children joyful. He does all that he can to make them happy. Likewise, God also desires that His children should walk before Him with a joyful heart. He has promised them joy—He will give it.[1] He has commanded it—we must take it and walk in it at all times.[2]

The reason for this is not difficult to find. Joy is always the evidence that something really satisfies me and has great value for me. Joy, more than anything else, recommends its cause to others. And joy in God is the strongest proof that I have in God what satisfies and satiates me. It shows that I do not serve Him with dread, or remain faithful only

---

[1]Ps. 89:16,17; Isa. 29:19; John 16:22; 1 Pet. 1:8

[2]Ps. 32:11; Isa. 12:5,6; 1 Thess. 5:16; Phil. 4:4

because He is my salvation. Joy is the mark of the truth, the worth of obedience, and shows whether I have pleasure in the will of God.[3] It is for this reason that joy in God is so acceptable to Him, so strengthening to believers themselves and to all who are exposed to the most eloquent testimony of what we think of God.[4]

In the Scriptures, light and joy are frequently connected with each other.[5] It is so in nature. The joyful light of the morning awakens the birds to their song and gladdens the watchers who, in the darkness, have longed for the day. It is the light of God's countenance that gives the Christian his joy. In fellowship with his Lord, he can, and always will, be happy. The love of the Father shines like the sun on His children.[6] When darkness comes over the soul, it is always through one of two things—through sin or through unbelief. Sin is darkness and makes life dark. Unbelief also makes life dark, for it turns us from Him, who alone is the light.

The question is sometimes asked, "Can the Christian always walk in the light?" The answer of our Lord is clear, "He that followeth Me shall *not* walk in darkness." It is sin, the turning from Jesus to our own way, that makes darkness. But at the moment we confess sin, and have it cleansed in the blood, we are again in the light.[7]

---

[3]Deut. 28:47; Ps. 11:9; 119:11

[4]Neh. 8:11; Ps. 68:4; Prov. 4:18

[5]Esth. 8:16; Prov. 13:9; 15:30; Isa. 60:20

[6]Ex. 10:23; 2 Sam. 23:4; Ps. 36:10; Isa. 60:1,20; 1 John 1:5; 4:16

[7]Josh 7:13; Isa. 58:10; 59:1,2,9; Matt. 15:14,16; 2 Cor. 6:14; Eph. 5:8,14; 1 Thess. 5:5; 1 John 2:10

Other times it is unbelief that causes darkness. When we look to ourselves and our strength, when we seek comfort in our own feelings, or our own works, then all becomes dark. As soon as we look to Jesus, to the fullness—the perfect provision for our needs that is in Him—all is light. He says, "I am the Light of the world: he that followeth Me shall not walk in darkness, but shall have the light of life." So long as I believe, I have light and joy.[8]

Christians, who want to walk according to the will of the Lord, hear what His Word says, "Finally, my brethren, rejoice in the Lord. Rejoice in the Lord always: again, I will say, Rejoice."[9] In the Lord Jesus there is unspeakable joy—full of glory. Believing in Him, rejoice in this. Live the life of faith. That life is salvation and glorious joy. A heart that gives itself undividedly to follow Jesus, that lives by faith in Him and His love, will have light and joy. Therefore, soul, only believe. Do not seek joy—in that case you will not find it, because you are seeking feeling. But seek Jesus, follow Jesus, believe in Jesus, and joy will be given to you. "Ye see him not, yet believing, rejoice with joy unspeakable and full of glory" (1 Peter 1:8).

Lord Jesus, You are the Light of the world, the radiance of the unapproachable light, in whom we see the light of God. From Your countenance radiates upon us the illumination of the knowledge of the love and glory of God. And You are ours, our light and our salvation. Teach us to believe more firmly that with You we can never walk in the darkness. Let joy in You be the proof that You are all to

[8]John 12:36; 11:40; Rom. 15:13; 1 Pet. 1:3
[9]Phil. 3:1; 4:4

*us and our strength to do all that You would have us
do. Amen.*

Notes

1. The joy that I have in anything is the measure of
its worth in my eyes—the joy in a person is the
measure of my pleasure in him; the joy in a work is
the measure of my pleasure in it. Joy in God and His
service is one of the surest signs of a healthy spiritual
life.

2. Joy is hindered by ignorance, when we do not
understand God and His love and the blessedness of
His service. Joy is hindered by unbelief, when we still
seek something in our own strength or feeling. Joy is
also hindered by double-heartedness, when we are
not willing to give up and lay aside everything for
Jesus.

3. Understand this saying, "He that seeks gladness
shall not find it; he that seeks the Lord and His will,
shall find gladness unsought." Think this over. He
who seeks joy as a thing of feeling, seeks himself. He
who wants happiness will not find it. He who forgets
himself to live in the Lord and His will, will be taught
of himself to rejoice in the Lord. It is God, God
Himself, who is the God of the joy of our gladness.
Seek God and you will have joy. You have then
simply to take and enjoy it by faith.

4. To thank God much for what He is and does, to
believe much in what God says and will do, is the
way to continual joy.

5. "The light of the eyes rejoiceth the heart" (Prov.
15:30). God has not intended that His children
should walk in the darkness. Satan is the prince of
the darkness. God is light. Christ is the light of the

world. We are children of the light, so let us walk in the light. Let us believe in the promise, "The Lord shall be to thee an everlasting light. Thy sun shall no more go down; for the Lord shall be thine everlasting light, and the days of thy mourning shall be ended" (Isa. 60:19,20).

Chapter 33
Chastisement

"Blessed is the man whom Thou chastenest, O Lord, and teachest out of Thy law; that Thou mayest give him rest from the days of adversity" Psalm 94:12,13.

"Before I was afflicted, I went astray; but now have I kept Thy word. . . . It is good for me that I have been afflicted; that I might learn Thy statutes" Psalm 119:67,71.

"He chastens us for our profit, that we may be partakers of His holiness" Hebrews 12:10.

"Count it all joy, my brethren, when ye fall into divers temptations; Knowing this, that the trying of your faith worketh patience" James 1:2,3.

Every child of God must at one time or another enter the school of trial. What the Scriptures teach us is confirmed by experience. And the Scriptures teach us further, that we are to count it a joy when God takes us into this school. It is a part of our heavenly blessedness to be educated and sanctified by the Father through chastisement.

Not that trial in itself brings a blessing.[1] Just as there is no profit in watering or plowing seedless ground, so there are children of God who enter into trial and have little blessing from it. The heart is softened for a time, but they do not know how to obtain an abiding blessing from it. They do not

---

[1] Isa. 5:3; Hos. 7:14,15; 2 Cor. 7:10

know what the Father has in mind for them in the school of trial.

In a good school four things are necessary—a definite aim, a good textbook, a capable teacher, and a willing pupil.

1. Let the aim of any trial be clear to you. Holiness is the highest glory of the Father and also of the child. He "chastens us for our profit that we may be partakers of *His holiness.*"[2] In trial, the Christian often wants to have only comfort. Or he seeks to be quiet and contented under the special chastisement. This is indeed the beginning—but the Father desires something else, something higher. He wants to make him *holy*, holy for his whole life. When Job said, "Blessed be the name of the Lord" (Job 1:21), this was still just the beginning of his school time. The Lord still had more to teach him. God desires to unite our will with His holy will, not only on the one point in which He is trying us, but in everything. God wants to fill us with His Holy Spirit—with His holiness. This is the aim of God. This must also be your aim in the school of trial.

2. Especially during this time of trial, let the Word of God be your reading book. Notice how God desires to teach us His Word in our trials and afflictions. The Word will reveal to you why the Father chastens you, how deeply He loves you in the midst of it, and how rich His promises of consolation are. Trial will give new glory to the promises of the Father. In chastisement, return to the Word for counsel.[3]

3. Let Jesus be your teacher. He Himself was

[2]Isa. 27:8,9; 1 Cor. 11:32; Heb. 2:10; 12:11
[3]Ps. 119:49,50,92,143; Isa. 40:1; 43:2; Heb. 12:10-13

sanctified by suffering. It was in suffering that He learned full obedience. He has a wonderfully sympathetic heart. Have much communion with Him. Do not seek your comfort from the words spoken to or with other men. *Give Jesus the opportunity of teaching you.* Speak and meditate often with Him in solitude.[4] The Father has given you the Word, the Spirit, and the Lord Jesus as your sanctification, so that you may be set apart for Him. Affliction and chastisement are meant to bring you to the Word— to Jesus Himself—so that He may make you a partaker of His holiness. It is in fellowship with Jesus that consolation comes of itself.[5]

4. Be a willing pupil. Acknowledge your ignorance. Do not think that you understand the will of God. Ask and expect that the Lord will teach you the lesson that you are to learn in affliction. To the meek there is the promise of teaching and wisdom. Seek to have the ear open, the heart very quiet and turned toward God. Know that it is the Father who has placed you in the school of trial. Yield yourself with all willingness to hear what He says, and to learn what He would teach you. He will bless you greatly in this.[6]

"Blessed is the man whom Thou chastenest, and teachest out of Thy law" (Psalm 94:12). "Count it all joy when ye fall into divers temptations....that ye may be perfect and entire, wanting nothing" (James 1:2,4). Regard the time of trial as a time of blessing, as a time of close communication with the Father, of being made a partaker of His holiness, and you will

---

[4]Isa. 26:16; 61:1,2; Heb. 2:10,17,18; 5:9

[5]2 Cor. 1:3,4; Heb. 13:5,6

[6]Ps. 25:9; 39:2,10; Isa. 50:4,5

also rejoicingly say, "It is good for me that I have been afflicted" (Psalm 119:71).

Father, what thanks I will express to You for the glorious light that Your Word casts upon the dark trials of this life. You will teach me by this means and make me a partaker of Your holiness. You have not considered the suffering and the death of Your beloved Son too much to bring holiness near to me. And I will be willing to endure Your chastisement to become a partaker of that holiness. Father, thanks be to You for Your precious work. Only fulfill Your counsel in me. Amen.

Notes

1. In chastisement it is first of all necessary that we should be possessed by the thought—this is the will of God. Although the trial comes through our own folly or the perversity of men, we must acknowledge that it is the will of God that we should be in that suffering by means of that folly or perversity. We see this clearly in Joseph and the Lord Jesus. Nothing will give us rest but the willing acknowledgment— this is the will of God.

2. The second thought is—God wills not only the trial, but also the consolation, the power, and the blessing in it. He who acknowledges the will of God in the chastisement itself is on the way to see and experience the accompaniments also as the will of God.

3. The will of God is as perfect as He Himself. Let us not be afraid to surrender ourselves to it. No one suffers loss by deeming the will of God unconditionally good.

4. This is holiness—to know and to adore the will

of God, to unite one's self wholly with it.

5. Do not seek comfort in trial in connection with men. Do not mingle too much with them. Rather, see to it that you deal with God and His Word. The object of trial is just to draw you away from what is earthly so that you may turn to God and give Him time to unite your will with His perfect will.

Chapter 34

Prayer

"Thou, when thou prayest, enter into thine inner chamber, and when thou hast shut thy door, pray to thy Father which is in secret, and thy Father which seeth in secret shall reward thee openly" Matthew 6:6.

The spiritual life with its growth depends a great deal on prayer. My life will flourish or decay according to how much or how little I pray, if I pray with pleasure or from duty, and if I pray according to the Word or according to my own inclination. In the word of Jesus quoted above, we have the principal ideas of true prayer.

Alone with God—that is the first thought. The door must be shut, with the world and man outside, because I am to hold communion with God undisturbed. When God met with His servants in the olden time, He took them alone.[1] Let the first thought in your prayer be—God and I are here in the chamber with each other. The power of your prayer will be in accordance with your conviction of the nearness of God.

In the presence of *your Father*—this is the second thought. You come to the inner chamber, because your Father with His love awaits you there. Although you are cold, dark, sinful—although it is doubtful whether you can pray at all—come,

---

[1]Gen. 18:22,23; 22:5; 32:24; Ex. 33:11

because the Father is there, and He looks upon you. Set yourself beneath the light of His eye. Believe in His tender, fatherly love, and out of this faith prayer will be born.[2]

Count certainly upon an answer—that is the third point in the word of Jesus. "Your Father will reward you openly." There is nothing which the Lord Jesus has spoken so positively about as the certainty of an answer to prayer. Review the promises.[3] Observe how constantly in the Psalms—that prayerbook of God's saints—God is called the God who hears prayer and gives answers.[4]

It may be that there is much in you that prevents the answer. Delay in the answer is a very blessed discipline. It leads to self-searching as to whether we are praying improperly, and whether our life is truly in harmony with our prayer. It leads to a purer exercise of faith.[5] It draws us into a closer and more persistent relationship with God. The sure confidence of an answer is the secret of powerful praying. Let us always keep this as the chief thing in prayer. When you pray, stop in the midst of your prayer to ask, "Do I believe that I am receiving what I pray for?" Let your faith receive and hold firm the answer as given. It will turn out according to your faith.[6]

Beloved young Christians, if there is one thing

[2]Matt. 6:8; 7:11

[3]Matt. 6:7,8; Mark 11:24; Luke 18:8; John 14:13,14; 15:7,16; 16:23,24

[4]Ps. 3:4; 4:3; 6:9; 10:17; 17:6; 20:2,7; 34:5,7,17,18; 38:15; 40:1,2; 65:2; 66:19

[5]Josh. 7:12; 1 Sam. 8:18; 14:37,38; 28:6,15; Prov. 21:13; Isa. 1:15; Mic. 3:4; Hag. 1:9; Jas. 1:6; 4:3; 5:16

[6]Ps. 145:9; Isa. 30:19; Jer. 33:3; Mal. 3:10; Matt. 9:29; 15:28; 1 John 3:22; 5:14,15

about which you must be conscientious, it is this —secret conversation with God. Your life is hidden with Christ in God. Everyday you must, in prayer, ask from above and by faith receive what you need for that day. Every day personal communion with the Father and the Lord Jesus must be renewed and strengthened. God is our salvation and our strength. Christ is our life and our holiness. Only in personal fellowship with the living God is our blessedness found.

Christian, pray much, pray continually, pray without ceasing. When you have no desire to pray, *go just then to the inner chamber.* Go as one who has nothing to bring to the Father, to set yourself before Him in faith in His love. Coming in that manner to the Father, and abiding before Him, is already a prayer which He understands. Be assured that to appear before God, however passively, always brings a blessing. The Father not only hears—He sees in secret, and He will reward openly.

My Father, You have so certainly promised in Your Word to hear the prayer of faith—give me the Spirit of prayer so that I may know how to offer that prayer. Graciously reveal to me Your wonderful, fatherly love. Make me aware of the complete blotting out of my sins in Christ, by which every hindrance in this direction is taken away. And reveal to me the intercession of the Spirit in me, by which my ignorance or weakness cannot deprive me of the blessing. Teach me with faith in You, the Trinity, to pray in fellowship with You. And confirm in me the strong, living certainty that I receive what I believingly ask. Amen.

Notes

1. The principal thing in prayer is faith. The whole of salvation, the whole of the new life is by faith, therefore also by prayer. There is all too much prayer that brings nothing, because there is little faith in it. Before I pray, and while I pray, and after I have prayed, I must ask, "Do I pray in faith?" I must say, "I believe with my whole heart."

2. To arrive at this faith we must take time in prayer. We must take the time to set ourselves silently and trustfully before God, and to become awake to His presence. We must take time to have our soul sanctified in fellowship with God. We must take time for the Holy Spirit to teach us to hold firm and to trustfully use the Word of promise. No earthly knowledge, no earthly possessions, no earthly food, no conversations with friends can we have without time—sufficient time. Let us not think to learn how to pray, how to enjoy the power and the blessedness of prayer, if we do not take time with God.

3. And then there must be not only time every day, but perseverance from day to day. Time is required to grow in the certainty that we are acceptable to the Father, and that our prayer has power, in the loving confidence which knows that our prayer is according to His will and is heard. We must not suppose that we know how to pray well enough, and can but ask and it is over. No, prayer is conversation and fellowship with God, in which God has time and opportunity to work in us, in which our souls die to their own will and power and become bound up and united with God.

4. For encouragement in persistent prayer, the

following instance may be of service. In an address delivered at Calcutta, George Muller said that in 1844 five persons were laid upon his heart, and that he began to pray for their conversion. Eighteen months passed by before the first was converted. He prayed five more years and the second was converted. After twelve and a half years, yet another was converted. At the time the address was given he had already prayed forty years for the other two, without letting a day go by, and they still were not converted. He was, nevertheless, full of courage in the sure confidence that these two would also be given him in answer to his prayer.

5. I have endeavored in thirty-one meditations to explain the principal points of the life of prayer in the book, *With Christ in the School of Prayer*.

Chapter 35
The Prayer Meeting

"Again I say unto you, that if two of you shall agree on earth as touching anything that they shall ask, it shall be done for them of My Father which is in heaven. For where two or three are gathered together in My name, there am I in the midst of them" Matthew 18:19,20.

The Lord Jesus has told us to go into the inner chamber and hold our personal conversation with God by praying privately—not to be seen by men. The very same voice tells us that we are also to pray in fellowship with one another.[1] And when He went to heaven, the birth of the Christian Church took place in a prayer meeting which one hundred and twenty men and women held for ten days.[2] The Day of Pentecost was the fruit of unanimous, persevering prayer.

Everyone desiring to please the Lord Jesus, longing for the gift of the Spirit—with power for their congregation or church—and wanting the blessing of fellowship with other children of God, should attach themselves to a prayer meeting and prove that the Lord will make good His Word, bestowing a special blessing upon it.[3] And let them take part in it, so that the prayer meeting may be such as the Lord presented it to us.

---

[1]Matt. 6:6; Luke 9:18,28
[2]Acts 1:14
[3]2 Chron. 20:4,17,18; Neh. 9:2,3; Joel 2:16,17; Acts 12:5

For a blessed prayer meeting, there must be, first of all, agreement concerning that which we desire. There must be something that we really desire to have from God. We are to be in harmony concerning this. There must be inner love and unity among the petitioners—all that is strife, envy, wrath, lovelessness, makes prayer powerless[4]—and then agreement on the definite object that is desired.[5] To achieve this, it is entirely proper that what people are to pray for should be stated in the prayer meeting. Whether one of the members wants to have his particular needs brought forward, or whether others would bring more general needs to the Lord—such as the conversion of the unconverted, the revival of God's children, the anointing of the teacher, the extension of the Kingdom—let the objects be announced beforehand. And let no one think that there is complete agreement whenever *one* is content to pray for these objects. No, we are all to take them into our heart and life, and to bring them continually before the Lord. We are to be inwardly eager that the Lord should give them. Then, we are on the way to the prayer which has power.

The second feature that characterizes a proper prayer meeting is the coming together in the name of Jesus with awareness of His presence. The Scripture says, "The name of the Lord is a strong tower: the righteous runneth into it, and is safe" (Proverbs 18:10). The name is the expression of the person. When they come together, believers are to enter into the name of Jesus, and to find within this name their fortress and abode. In this name, they mingle with

---

[4] Ps. 133:1,3; Jer. 50:4,5; Matt. 5:23,24; 18:19,20; Mark 11:25
[5] Jer. 32:39; Acts 4:24

one another before the Father, and out of this name they pray. This name also makes them truly one with each other. And when they are thus in this name, the living Lord Himself is in their midst. He says that this is the reason why the Father certainly hears them.[6] They are in Him, and He is in them. Out of Him they pray, and their prayer comes before the Father in His power. Let the name of Jesus truly be the point of union—the meeting-place—in our prayer meetings. Then we will be conscious that He is in our midst.

Then there is the third feature of united prayer of which the Lord has told us—our request will certainly be done by the Heavenly Father. The prayer will certainly be answered. We may well cry out in these days, "Where is the Lord God of Elijah?" (2 Kings 2:14), for He was a God that answered. "The God that answereth by fire, let Him be God," said Elijah to the people (1 Kings 18:24). And he said to God, "Hear me, O Lord, hear me, that this people may know that Thou art the Lord God" (1 Kings 18:37).[7] When we are content with much praying, with continuous praying, without answer, then little answer will be given. But when we understand that the answer is the principal thing—the token of God's pleasure in our prayer—and are not willing to be content without it, we will discover what our prayer lacks and begin to pray that an answer may come. And we may firmly believe this—the Lord takes delight in answering. It is a joy to Him when His people so enter into the name of Jesus, and pray out

---

[6] John 14:13,14; 15:7,16; 16:23,24
[7] Jas. 5:16

of it, that He can give them what they desire.[8]

Children of God, however young and weak you may still be, here is one of the institutions prepared for you by the Lord Jesus Himself to supply you with help in prayer. Let everyone make use of the prayer meeting. Let everyone go in a praying and believing frame of mind, seeking the name and the presence of the Lord. Let everyone seek to live and pray with his brothers and sisters. And let everyone expect to surely see glorious answers to prayer.

Blessed Lord Jesus, who has given us a commandment to pray—in the solitary inner chamber as well as in public fellowship with one another—let the one habit always make the other more precious as a complement and confirmation. Let the inner chamber prepare us and awaken the need for union with Your people in prayer. Let Your presence there be our blessedness. And let fellowship with Your people strengthen us to expect and receive answers. Amen.

Notes

1. There are many places in our country where prayer meetings might be a great blessing. A Christian man or woman, who once a week, or on Sunday, gathers together the inhabitants on a farm, or the neighbors of two or three homes that are not far from one another, might be able to attain great blessing. Let every believing reader of this portion inquire if there is not already some such need in his neighborhood. Let him make a beginning in the name of the Lord. Let me therefore earnestly put the question to every reader—is there a prayer meeting

---

[8]Acts 12:5; 2 Cor. 1:11; Jas. 4:3; 5:16,17

in your district? Do you faithfully take part in it? Do you know what it is to come together with the children of God in the name of Jesus, to experience His presence and His hearing of prayer?

2. You could obtain a book on prayer with suitable passages to be read aloud in such gatherings. Or read this book, *The New Life*, which will certainly give material for prayer.

3. Will the prayer meeting do harm to the inner chamber? is a question sometimes asked. My experience is just the opposite of this result. The prayer meeting is a school of prayer. The weak learn from more advanced petitioners. Material for prayer is given, as is the opportunity for self-searching and encouragement to more prayer.

4. If only it were more common in prayer meetings for people to speak of definite objects for which to pray—things in which one can definitely and trustfully look out for an answer, and concerning which one can know when an answer comes. Such announcements would greatly further agreement and believing expectation.

Chapter 36

The Fear Of The Lord

"Blessed is the man that feareth the Lord. He shall not be afraid of evil tidings. His heart is established, he shall not be afraid" Psalm 102:1,7,8.

"So the Church, walking in the fear of the Lord and in the comfort of the Holy Ghost, was multiplied" Acts 9:31.

The Scriptures use the word "fear" in a twofold way. In some places it speaks of "fear" as something wrong and sinful, and in the strongest terms it forbids us to "fear."[1] The word occurs in almost one hundred places—"Fear not." In many other places, on the contrary, fear is praised as one of the surest signs of true godliness, acceptable to the Lord, and full of His blessing for us.[2] The people of God bear the name—those who fear the Lord. The distinction between these two lies in this simple fact—the one is unbelieving fear, the other is believing.

Where fear is found connected with lack of trust in God, there it is sinful and very hurtful.[3] The fear, on the other hand, that is coupled with trust and hope in God is, for the spiritual life, entirely indispensable. The fear that man has for what is worldly is condemned. The fear that with childlike confidence and

---

[1]Gen. 15:1; Isa. 8:13; Jer. 32:40; Rom. 8:15; 1 Pet. 3:14; 1 John 4:18

[2]Ps. 22:23,25; 33:18; 112:1; 115:13; Prov. 28:14

[3]Matt. 8:26; Rev. 21:8

love honors the Father is commanded.[4] It is the believing fear of the Lord—not as a slave, but as a child—that the Scriptures present as a source of blessing and power. He who fears the Lord will fear nothing else. The fear of the Lord will be the beginning of all wisdom. The fear of the Lord is the sure way to the enjoyment of God's favor and protection.[5]

There are some Christians who, by their upbringing, are led into the reverent fear of the Lord even before they come to faith. This is a very great blessing. Parents can give a child no greater blessing than to bring him up in the fear of the Lord. When those who are thus brought up are brought to faith, they have a great advantage. They are, as it were, prepared to walk in the joy of the Lord. When, on the contrary, others that have not had this preparation come to conversion, they need special teaching and vigilance, in order to pray for and awaken this holy fear.

This fear is composed of many great elements. The principal are the following:

Holy reverence and awe before the glorious majesty of God and before His almighty holiness. These guard against the superficiality that forgets who God is and takes no pains to honor Him as God.[6]

Deep humility that is afraid of itself, and couples deep confidence in God with an entire distrust in itself. Conscious weakness that knows the sublety of its own heart always dreads doing anything contrary

---

[4]Ps. 33:18; 147:11; Luke 12:4,7
[5]Ps. 56:4,11; Prov. 1:7; 9:10; 10:27; 19:23; Acts 9:31; 2 Cor. 7:1
[6]Job 42:6; Ps. 5:7; Isa. 6:3,5; Hab. 2:20: Zeph. 2:3

to the will or honor of God. But just because he fears God, such a believer firmly depends on Him for protection. And this same humility inspires him in all his dealings with his fellow men.[7]

Cautiousness or vigilance. With holy forethought, it seeks to know the correct path, to watch against the enemy, and to guard against all frivolity or hastiness in speech, resolve, and conduct.[8]

Holy zeal and courage in watching and striving. The fear of displeasing the Lord by not conducting one's self as His servant in all things encourages faithfulness in that which is least expected. The fear of the Lord takes away all other fear and gives inconceivable courage in the certainty of victory.[9]

And out of this reverent fear is then born *joy.* "Rejoice with trembling" (Psalm 2:11). The fear of the Lord gives joy its depth and stability. Fear is the root, joy is the fruit. The deeper this fear, the higher the joy. On this account, it is said, "Ye that fear the Lord, praise Him" (Psalm 22:23). "Ye that fear the Lord, bless the Lord" (Psalm 135:20).

Young disciples of Christ, hear the voice of your Father. "Fear the Lord, ye His saints." Let reverent fear of the Lord, and dread of all that might displease or grieve Him, fill you. Then you will never have to fear any evil. He who fears the Lord and seeks to do all that pleases Him, for him God will also do all that he desires. The childlike, believing fear of God will lead you into the love and joy of God, while slavish, unbelieving, cowardly fear is utterly cast out.

---

[7]Luke 18:2,4; Rom. 11:20; 1 Pet. 3:2,5
[8]Prov. 2:5,11; 8:12,13; 13:13; 16:6; Luke 1:74
[9]Deut. 6:2; Isa. 12:2

O God, unite my heart for the reverent fear of Your name. May I always be among those who fear the Lord, and who hope in His mercy. Amen.

Notes

1. What are some of the blessings of the reverent fear of God? (Ps. 31:20; 115:13; 127:11; 114:19; Prov. 1; 7; 8; 13; 14; 27; Acts 10:35.)

2. What are the reasons why we are to fear God? (Deut. 10:17,20,21; 1 Sam. 12:24; Jer. 5:22; 10:6,7; Matt. 10:28; Rev. 15:4.)

3. It is especially the knowledge of God in His greatness, power, and glory that will fill the soul with fear. But for this purpose we must set ourselves silently before Him and take time for our soul to come under the impression of His majesty.

4. "He delivered me from all my fears" (Ps. 34:4). Does this apply to every different sort of fear by which you are hindered? There is the fear of man (Isa. 2:12,13; Heb. 13:16); the fear of heavy trial (Isa. 11:1,2); the fear of our own weakness (Isa. 12:10); the fear for the work of God (1 Chron. 28:20); the fear of death (Ps. 23:4).

5. Do you now understand the word, "Blessed is the man that fears the Lord. His heart is established, he shall not be afraid...."?

Chapter 37
Undivided Consecration

"And Ittai answered the king and said, As the Lord liveth, surely in what place my lord the king shall be, whether in death or life, even there also will thy servant be" 2 Samuel 15:21.

"Whosoever he be of you that forsaketh not all that he hath, he cannot be My disciple" Luke 14:33.

"Come out from among them, and be ye separate, saith the Lord, and touch not the unclean thing; and I will receive you, and will be a Father unto you" 2 Corinthians 6:17,18.

"I count all things but loss for the excellency of the knowledge of Christ Jesus my Lord" Philippians 3:8.

We have already said that surrender to the Lord is something that always obtains newer and deeper significance for the Christian. When this takes place, he comes to understand how this surrender involves nothing less than a complete and undivided consecration to live only, always, and wholly for Jesus. As entirely as the temple was dedicated to the service of God alone, so that everyone knew that it existed for that purpose only, likewise, you belong entirely to your Lord. As entirely as the offering on the altar could be used only according to God's command, and no one had a right to dispose of one portion other than He had said, your consecration to Him must be equally as undivided. God continually reminded Israel that He had redeemed them to be

His possession.[1] Let us see what this implies.

There is *personal attachment to Jesus*, and fellowship with Him in secret. He will be—He must be—the beloved, the desire, the joy of our souls. We are to be first consecrated to the service of Jesus as our Friend and King, our Redeemer and God.[2] It is only the spiritual impulse of a personal, cordial love that can place us in a condition for a life of complete consecration. Continually Jesus used the words, "For My sake," "Follow Me," "My disciple." He Himself must be the central point.[3] He gave Himself. The characteristic of a disciple is to desire to have Him, to love and to depend on Him.

Then there is *public confession*. What has been given to any one will be acknowledged by all as his property. His possessions are his glory. When the Lord Jesus manifests His great grace to a soul in redeeming it, He desires that the world should see and know it. He wants to be known and honored as its proprietor. He desires that everyone who belongs to Him would confess Him and proclaim that Jesus is King.[4] Without this public confession, the surrender is but a half-hearted one. As a part of this public confession, it is also required that we join His people and acknowledge them as our people. The one new commandment that the Lord gave—the sure sign by which all should recognize that we are His disciples—is brotherly love. Although the children of God in a locality are few or despised or full of imperfection, you are to join them. Love them. Hold

---

[1]Ex. 19:4,5; Lev. 1:8,9; Deut. 7:6; Rom. 12:1; 1 Cor. 3:16,17

[2]John 14:21; 15:14,15; 21:17; Gal. 2:20

[3]Matt. 10:32,33,37,38,40; Luke 14:26,27,33; 18:22

[4]Ex. 33:16; Josh. 24:25; John 8:35

fellowship with them. Attach yourself to them in prayer meetings and otherwise. Love them fervently. Brotherly love has wonderful power to open the heart for the love and the indwelling of God.[5]

To complete your consecration, there also must be separation from sin and the world. Do not touch the unclean thing. Know that the world is under the power of the Evil One. Do not ask how much of it you can retain without being lost. Do not always ask what is sin and what is lawful. Even that which is lawful the Christian must often make a willing renunciation of, in order to be able to live wholly for his God.[6] Abstinence even from lawful things is often indispensable for the full imitation of the Lord Jesus. Live as one who is really separated for God and His holiness. He who renounces everything, who counts everything loss for Jesus' sake, will receive a hundredfold even in this life.[7]

And what I separate from everything, I will use. Entire consecration has its eye on making us useful and fit for God and His service. Let there not be the least amount of doubt as to whether God has need of you and will make you a great blessing. Only give yourself unreservedly into His hands. Present yourself to Him, so that He may fill you with His blessing, His love, His Spirit. You *will* be a blessing.[8]

Let no one fear that this demand for a complete consecration is too high for him. You are not under

---

[5]Ruth 1:16; John 15:12; Rom. 12:5; 1 Cor. 12:20,21; Eph. 4:14,16; 1 Pet. 1:22
[6]1 Cor. 8:13; 9:25,27; 10:23; 2 Cor. 6:16,17; 2 Tim. 2:4
[7]Gen. 22:13,17; 2 Chron. 25:9; Luke 18:29,30; John 12:24,25; Phil. 3:8
[8]2 Tim. 2:21

the law which demands, but gives no power. You are under grace, which itself works what it requires.[9] Like the first surrender, every fresh dedication is yielded to Jesus, whom the Father has given to do all things for you. Consecration is an act of faith, a part of the glorious life of faith. It is on this account that you have to say—it is not I, but the grace of God in me, that will do it. I live only by faith in Him who works in me the willing as well as the performance.[10]

Blessed Lord, open the eyes of my heart so that I may see how completely You would have me for Yourself. May you be, in the hidden depths of my heart, the one power that keeps me occupied and holds me in possession. Let all know You are my King, that I ask only for Your will. In my separation from the world, in my surrender to Your people and to Your will, let it be manifest that I am wholly, yes wholly, the Lord's. Amen.

Notes

1. There is almost no point of the Christian life in connection with which I should more desire to urge you to pray to God that He may enlighten your eyes, than this of the entire consecration that God desires. In myself and others, I discover that with our own thoughts we can form no conception of how completely God Himself wants to take possession of our will and live in us. The Holy Spirit must reveal this in us. Only then indeed does a conviction arise of how little we understand this. We are not to think, "I see truly how entirely I must live for God, but I cannot accomplish this." No, we are to say, "I am still blind;

---

[9] 2 Cor. 9:8; 2 Thess. 1:11,12
[10] 1 Cor. 15:10; Gal. 2:20; Phil 2:13

I have still no view of what is the glory of a life in which God is all. Once I see that, I would strongly desire and believe that not I, but God, should work it in me."

2. Let there be no doubt in your mind as to whether you have given yourself to God, to live wholly and only as His. Express this conviction before him often. Acknowledge that you do not yet see or understand what it means, but abide by this, that you desire it to be so. Rely on the Holy Spirit to seal you, to stamp you as God's entire possession. Even if you stumble and discover self-will, hold your integrity tightly, and trustfully affirm that the deep, firm choice of your heart is to live for God in all things.

3. Always keep before your eyes that the power to give all to the Lord, and to be all for the Lord, arises from the fact that He has given all for you, that He is all for you. Faith in what He did for you is the power of what you do for Him.

Chapter 38
Assurance of Faith

"Abraham staggered not at the promise of God through unbelief, but was strong in faith, giving glory to God, and being fully persuaded that, what He had promised, He was able also to perform" Romans 4:20,21.

"My little children, let us not love in word, neither in tongue; but in deed and truth. Hereby we know that we are of the truth, and shall assure our hearts before Him" 1 John 3:18,19.

"And hereby we know that He abideth in us, by the Spirit which He hath given us" 1 John 3:24.

Every child of God needs the assurance of faith—the full certainty of faith—that the Lord has received him and made him His child. The Holy Scriptures always speak to Christians as those who know that they are redeemed and as those who know they are now children of God and have received eternal life.[1] How can a child love or serve his father while he is uncertain whether his father will really acknowledge him as a child? We have already spoken on this point in a previous chapter, but often, by ignorance or distrust, a Christian again comes into darkness. For this reason, we will now deal with it once again with a set purpose.

Scripture names three things by which we have our certainty. First, there is *faith* in the Word. After

---

[1]Deut. 26:17,18; Isa. 44:5; Gal. 4:7; 1 John 5:12

that, there are *works*. And then, in and with both of these, there is *the Holy Spirit*.

First, *faith* in the Word. Abraham is to us the great example of faith and of the assurance of faith. And what then says the Scripture about the certainty that he had? He was fully assured that what God had promised He was also able to perform. His expectation was only from God, and what God had promised. He relied upon God to do what He had said. The promise of God was for him his only, but sufficient, assurance of faith.[2]

There are many young Christians who think that faith in the Word is not sufficient to give full assurance. They would gladly have something more. They imagine that assurance—a sure inward feeling or conviction—is what is given above or outside of faith. This is wrong. As I have need of nothing more than the word of a trustworthy man to give me complete certainty, so must the Word of God be my assurance. People err because they seek something in themselves and in their feeling. No, the whole of salvation comes from God. The soul must not be occupied with itself or its work, but with God. He who forgets himself to hear what God says, and to rely on His promise as something worthy of credit, has the fullest assurance of faith.[3] He does not doubt the promises but is strong in faith. He gives God the glory and is fully assured that what was promised, God is also able to perform.

Then the Scripture also names *works*—by unfeigned love we will assure our hearts.[4] Carefully

[2]John 3:33; 5:24; Acts 27:25; Rom. 4:21,22; 1 John 5:10,11
[3]Num. 23:19; Ps. 89:35; Isa. 54:9
[4]1 John 3:18,19

observe this—assurance by faith in the promise, without works, comes first. The godless man who receives grace knows this only from the Word. But then, later on, assurance is to follow from works. "By works was faith made perfect" (James 2:22).[5] The tree is planted in faith, without fruits. But when the time of fruit arrives, and no fruit appears, then I may doubt. At the outset, the more clearly I hold the assurance of faith on the Word alone—without works—the more certainly works will follow.

And both assurance by faith and by works come by *the Spirit*. A child of God has the heavenly certification that he is the Lord's.[6] This comes, not by the Word alone, and not by works as something that he does himself, but by the Word as the instrument of the Spirit and by works as the fruit of the Spirit.

Let us believe in Jesus as our life and abide in Him, and assurance of faith will never be lacking in us.

Father, teach me to find my assurance of faith in a life with You, in a cordial reliance upon Your promises, and in cordial obedience to Your commands. Let Your Holy Spirit also witness with my spirit that I am a child of God. Amen.

Notes

1. The importance of the assurance of faith lies in the fact that I cannot possibly love or serve, as a child, a God of whom I do not know whether He loves and acknowledges me as His child.

2. The whole Bible is one great proof for the assurance of faith. Just because it speaks of itself so,

[5]John 15:10,14; Gal. 5:6; 1 John 3:14
[6]John 4:13; Rom. 8:13,14; 1 John 3:24

it is not always regarded as such. Abraham and Moses knew that God had redeemed them—for this reason they had to serve God. How much more must this be the case in the greater redemption of the New Testament? All the Epistles are written to men of whom it is presupposed that they know and confess that they are redeemed, holy children of God.

3. Faith and obedience are inseparable, as root and fruit. First, there must be the root, and it must have time to be without fruit. Then later on the fruits come. First, assurance without fruits by living faith in the Word. Then, further assurance from fruits. It is in a life with Jesus that assurance of faith is exalted firmly above all doubt.

4. Assurance of faith is helped by confession. What I express becomes for me more evident. I am bound to confirm it.

5. It is at the feet of Jesus, looking up into His friendly countenance, listening to His loving promises, in fellowship with Jesus Himself in prayer, that all doubtfulness of mind falls away. Go there for the full assurance of faith.

Chapter 39
Conformity To Jesus

"Predestined to be conformed to the image of His Son" Romans 8:29.

"I have given you an example, that ye should do as I have done to you" John 13:15.

The Bible speaks of two types of conformity, a twofold likeness which we bear. We may be conformed to the world or to Jesus. The one excludes and drives out the other. More than anything else, conformity to Jesus will be secretly prevented by conformity to the world. And conformity to the world can be overcome by nothing but conformity to Jesus.

Young Christian, the new life of which you have become partaker is the life of God in heaven. That life is revealed and made visible in Christ. What the workings and fruits of eternal life were in Jesus, they will also be in you. In His life you get to see what eternal life will work in you. It cannot be otherwise. If for this reason you surrender yourself unreservedly to Jesus and the dominion of eternal life, it will bring forth in you a walk of wonderful conformity to that of Jesus.[1]

Two things, especially, are necessary for a true imitation of Jesus in His example and for growth in inward conformity to Him. These are, *a clear insight* that I am really called to this, and *a firm trust* that it

---

[1]Matt. 20:27,28; Luke 6:40; John 6:57; 1 John 2:6; 4:17

is possible for me.

One of the greatest hindrances in the spiritual life is that we do not know—we do not see—what God desires that we should be.[2] Our understanding is still enlightened so little, and we still have so many of our own human thoughts and imaginations about the true service of God. We know so little of waiting for the Spirit who alone can teach us. We do not acknowledge that even the clearest words of God do not have for us the meaning and power that God desires. And as long as we do not spiritually discern what likeness to Jesus is, and how utterly we are called to live like Him, little can be said of true conformity. If only we could understand how very much we need divine instruction on this point.[3]

For this reason, let us earnestly examine the Scriptures in order to know what God says and desires about our conformity to Christ.[4] Let us unceasingly ponder such words of Scripture, and keep our heart in contact with them. Let it remain fixed with us that we have given ourselves wholly to the Lord—to be all that He desires. Let us trustfully pray that the Holy Spirit would inwardly enlighten us and bring us to a full awareness of the life of Jesus, so far as can be seen in a believer.[5] The Spirit will convince us that we, no less than Jesus, are absolutely called to live only for the will and glory of the Father. We are called to be in the world even as He is.

The other thing that we have need of is the belief

---

[2] Luke 24:16; 1 Cor. 3:1,2; Heb. 5:11,12
[3] 1 Cor. 2:12,13; Eph. 1:17-20
[4] John 13:15; 15:10,12; 17:18; Eph 5:2; Phil. 2:5; Col. 3:13
[5] 1 Cor. 11:1; 2 Cor. 3:18

that it is really possible for us to bear the image of our Lord. Unbelief is the cause of weakness. We can put this matter another way. We think that because we are powerless, we dare not believe that we can be conformed to our Lord. This thought is in conflict with the Word of God. We do not have it in our own power to carry ourselves after the image of Jesus. No, He is our head and our life. He lives in us and will have His life work from within outwards—with divine power through the Holy Spirit.[6]

Yet this cannot be separate from our faith. Faith is the consent of the heart, the surrender to Him to work, and the reception of His working. "Be it unto you according to your faith" (Matthew 9:29) is one of the fundamental laws of the Kingdom of God.[7] It is incredible what power unbelief has in hindering the working and the blessing of Almighty God. The Christian who wants to become conformed to Christ must cherish the firm trust that this blessing is within his reach and is entirely within the range of possibility. He must learn to look to Jesus as Him in whom, by the grace of God, he can be truly conformable. He must believe that the same Spirit that was in Jesus is also in him. He must believe that the same Father that led and strengthened Jesus also watches over him, and that the same Jesus that lived on earth now lives in him. He must cherish the strong assurance that the Trinity is at work in changing him into the image of the Son.[8]

He who believes this will receive it. It will not be without much prayer. It will especially require cease-

[6]John 14:23; 2 Cor. 13:3; Eph. 3:17,18
[7]Zech. 1:6; Matt. 18:19; Luke 1:37,45; 18:27; Gal. 2:20
[8]John 14:20; 17:19; Rom. 8:2; 2 Cor. 3:18; Eph. 1:19

less communion with the Father and Jesus. Yet he who desires it, and is willing to give time and sacrifice to it, certainly receives it.

Son of God, radiance of the glory of God, the very Image of His substance, I must be changed into Your image. In You I see the image and the likeness of God in which we were created, in which we are by You created anew. Lord Jesus, let conformity to You be the one desire, the one hope of my soul. Amen.

Notes

1. Conformity to Jesus—we think that we understand the Word, but how little do we comprehend that God really expects us to live even as Jesus did. It requires much time with Him, in prayer and pondering of His example, to correctly understand it. The writer of these precepts has written a book on this theme, has often spoken of it, and yet he sometimes feels as if he must cry out—Is it really true? Has God indeed called us to live even as Jesus?

2. Conformity to the world is strengthened especially by association with it. It is in fellowship with Jesus that we will adopt His mode of thinking, His disposition, His manners.

3. The main feature of the life of Jesus is that He surrendered Himself wholly to the Father in behalf of man. The chief feature of conformity to Him is the offering up of ourselves to God for the redemption and blessing of the lost.

4. The chief feature of His inner disposition was childlikeness—absolute dependence on the Father,

great willingness to be taught, cheerful preparedness to do the will of the Father. Be especially like Him in this.

Chapter 40
Conformity To The World

"I beseech you, brethren, that ye present your bodies a living sacrifice, holy, acceptable to God. And be not conformed to this world: but be ye transformed by the renewing of your mind, that ye may prove what is the good and acceptable, and perfect, will of God" Romans 12:1,2.

Do not be conformed to this world. But what is conformity to the world? The opposite of conformity to Jesus, for Jesus and the world stand directly opposed to each other. The world crucified Him. He and His disciples are not of the world. The spirit of this world and the Spirit of God exclude each other. The world cannot receive the Spirit of God, for it does not see Him and does not know Him.[1]

And what is the spirit of this world? The spirit of this world is the disposition which encourages mankind to continue in their natural condition, where the Spirit of God has not yet renewed them. The spirit of this world comes from the Evil One—the prince of this world—and has dominion over all who are not renewed by the Spirit of God.[2]

And in what does the spirit of this world, or conformity to it, manifest itself? The Word of God gives the answer, "All that is in the world, the lust of

---

[1]John 14:17; 17:14,16; 1 Cor. 2:6,8

[2]John 14:30; 16:11; 1 Cor. 2:12

the flesh, and the lust of the eyes, and the pride of life, is not of the Father, but is of the world" (1 John 2:16). The three chief forms of the spirit of the world are; the craving for pleasure or the desire *to enjoy* the world, the craving for property or the desire *to possess* the world, and the craving for glory or the desire *to be honored* in the world.[3]

And these three are one in root and essence. The spirit of this world is—that man makes himself his own end. He makes himself the central point of the world. All creation, so far as he has power over it, must serve him; he seeks his life in the visible. This is the spirit of the world—to seek one's self and the visible.[4] And the Spirit of Jesus is—to live not for one's self and not for the visible, but for God and the things that are invisible.[5]

It is a very terrible and serious thought that one can live a busy, fashionable life—free from obvious sin or unrighteousness—and yet remain a friend to the world, and therefore an adversary to God.[6]

We are conformed to this world if our care for the earthly—for what we eat and drink, for what we possess or may possess, and for what we have brought forth in the earth and have made to increase—is the chief element in our life. It is a terrible and very serious thought that one can maintain the appearance of a Christian life—think that one is trusting in Christ—while yet living with the world for self and the visible.[7] For this reason the com-

---

[3] 1 John 2:15,16
[4] John 5:44
[5] 2 Cor. 4:13; 5:7,15
[6] Jas. 4:4
[7] Matt. 6:32,33

mand comes to all Christians with great emphasis—
Be conformed, not to this world, but to Jesus.

And how can I not come to be conformed to the
world? Read our text over again with consideration.
There we read two things. One, it is those who have
presented their bodies to God as a sacrifice on the
altar that have it said to them—Be not conformed to
the world. Offer yourself to God—that is conformity
to Jesus. Live every day as one who is offered up to
God, crucified in Christ to the world. Then you will
not be conformed to the world.[8]

Then, two, it says: Be transformed by the renewing of your mind, that ye may prove what is the
perfect will of God. There must be a continuous
growing renewal of our mind. This takes place by the
Holy Spirit, when we let ourselves be led by Him.
Then we learn to spiritually judge what is according
to the will of God and what is according to the spirit
of the world. A Christian who strives after the progressive renewal of his whole mind will not be conformed to the world. The Spirit of God makes him
conformed to Jesus.[9]

Christians, please believe that Jesus has obtained
for you the power to overcome the world, with its
deep hidden seductions to living for ourselves.
Believe this. Believe in Him as Victor and that you
also have the victory.[10]

*Precious Lord, we have presented ourselves to
You as living sacrifices. We have offered up ourselves to God. We are not of the world, even as You
are not of the world. Lord, let our mind be enlight-*

---

[8] Gal. 6:14
[9] 2 Cor. 6:14,16; Eph. 5:17; Heb. 5:14
[10] John 16:33; 1 John 5:4,5

*ened by the renewing of the Holy Spirit, so that we
may rightly see what the spirit of this world is. And
let it be seen in us that we are not of the world, but
are conformed to Jesus. Amen.*

Notes

1. *Worldly pleasures.* Is dancing sin? What harm
is there in playing billiards? One has sometimes
wished that there were in the Scriptures a distinct
law to forbid such things. God has intentionally not
given this. If there were such a law, it would only
make men outwardly spiritual. God puts each one
on trial as to whether his inner disposition is worldly
or heavenly. Learn Romans 12 verses 1 and 2 by
heart and ask the Spirit of God to make it living in
you. The Christian who offers himself up to God and
becomes transformed by the renewing of the mind to
prove the perfect will of God will speedily learn
whether he may dance or play billiards. The Christian who is afraid only of hell, but not of conformity
to the world, cannot see what the Spirit of God gives
His children to see.

2. It is remarkable that the trinity of the god of this
world, in John's Epistle, is seen as well in the temptation in Paradise as in that of the Lord Jesus.
The lust of the flesh:

The woman saw that the tree was good for food
(Gen. 3:6).

Command that those stones be made bread (Matt.
4:3).

The lust of the eyes:

And that it was pleasant to the eyes (Gen. 3:6).

The devil showeth Him all the kingdoms of the
world (Matt. 4:8).

And the vainglory of life:

And that the tree was to be desired to make one wise (Gen. 3:6).

Cast Thyself down (Matt. 4:6).

3. Consider what I say to you—it is only conformity to Jesus that will keep out conformity to the world. Let conformity to Jesus be the study and the endeavor of your soul.

Chapter 41

The Lord's Day

"And God blessed the seventh day, and sanctified it: because that in it he had rested from all His work which God had created" Genesis 2:3.

"On that day, the first day of the week, Jesus came and stood in the midst, and saith unto them, Peace be unto you" John 20:19.

"I was in the Spirit on the Lord's day" Revelation 1:10.

Man lives under the law of time. He must have time for what he wants to do or obtain. In a wonderful way God gives him time for communion with Himself. One day in seven God separated for fellowship with Himself.

The great object of God's gift of this day is that it may serve as a sign that God desires to sanctify man.[1] Endeavor to understand well the word "holy." It is one of the most important words in the Bible.

God is the Holy One. By revealing Himself, God communicates His holiness to that which is holy. We know that the temple was holy, because God dwelt there. God had taken possession of it. He gave Himself to dwell there. In this way, God also wants to sanctify man. He wants to take possession of him and fill him with Himself—with His own life, His disposition, His holiness. For this reason, God took possession of the seventh day, appropriating it to Himself. He sanctified it. He also calls man to sanc-

---

[1]Ex. 31:13,17; Ezek. 20:12,20

tify it and to acknowledge it as the Lord's day—the day of the Lord's presence and special working. He who does this—who sanctifies this day—will be sanctified by Him, as God has promised. (Read with attention, Exodus 31:12-17, especially verse 13.)

God blessed the seventh day by sanctifying it. The blessing of God is the power of life, lodged by Him in everything. He blesses grass and cattle and man with the power to multiply.[2] And so He lodged in the seventh day a power to bless, and the promise that everyone who sanctifies this day will be sanctified and blessed by it. We must accustom ourselves to always think of the Sabbath as a blessed day that certainly brings blessing. The blessing bound up with it is very great.[3]

There is still a third word that is used when speaking of the Sabbath. "God rested on the seventh day," and, as it stands in Exodus, "was refreshed" or gladdened. God will sanctify and bless us by introducing us into His rest. He wants to bring us to see that we are not to burden ourselves with our cares and weaknesses. We are to rest in Him, in His finished work, in His rest, which He takes because all is in order. This rest is not the outward termination of employments. No, it is the rest of faith, by which we cease from our works as God did from His, because all is finished. Into this rest we enter by faith in the finished work of Jesus, in surrender to be sanctified by God.[4]

The seventh day is changed into the first day of the week because Jesus finished the second creation in

---

[2]Gen. 1:22,28; 22:17
[3]Isa. 56:4-7; 58:13,14
[4]Heb. 4:3,10

His resurrection, and we enter into life and rest by the power of His resurrection. There is no specific command on this point. In the New Testament, the Spirit takes the place of the law. The Spirit of the Lord led His disciples to the celebration of this day. It was the day, not only on which the Lord was raised, but also on which, in all likelihood, the Spirit was poured out. It was the day not only on which the Lord manifested Himself during the forty days, but on which the Spirit also specially worked.[5]

The chief lessons that we have to learn about this day are the following:

The principal aim of the Sabbath is to make you holy, as God is holy. God would have you holy—this is glory, this is blessedness—this is His blessing, this His rest. God would have you holy, filled with Himself and His holiness.[6]

In order to sanctify you, God must have you with Him, in His presence and fellowship. You are to come away from all your struggling and working to rest with Him. You are to rest quietly, without exertion or anxiety, in the certainty that the Son has finished everything, that the Father cares for you in everything, and that the Spirit will work everything in you. God can reveal Himself in the holy rest of a soul that is converted to God, remains silent before His presence to hear what He speaks to him, and depends on God to achieve all.[7] It is thus that He sanctifies us.

We sanctify the day of rest, first by withdrawing from all external business and distraction. Then, by

[5]John 20:1,19,26; Acts 1:8; 20:7; 1 Cor. 16:2; Rev. 1:10
[6]Ex. 29:43,45; Ezek. 37:27,28; 1 Pet. 1:15,16
[7]Ps. 62:2,6; Hab. 2:20; Zech. 2:13; John 19:30

employing it especially as God's day—belonging to the Lord—for what He destined it to be, fellowship with Himself.

Take care that you do not use the day of rest only as a day for the public observance of divine worship. It is especially in private personal communion that God can bless and sanctify you. In the church, the understanding is kept active, and you have the ordinances of preaching, united prayer, and praise to keep you occupied. But there we do not always know whether the heart is really dealing with God—is taking delight in Him. This takes place in solitude. Accustom yourself, then, to be alone with the Lord your God. Not only speak to Him, but let Him speak to you. Let your heart be the temple in whose holy silence His voice is heard. Rest in God. Then God will say of your heart: This is my rest, here will I dwell.[8]

Young Christian, hold in high regard the holy, the blessed day of rest. Long for it. Thank God for it. Keep it very holy. And, above all, let it be a day of inner fellowship with your God—a living conversation with His love.

Holy God, I thank You for the holy day which You give me as a token that You will sanctify me. Lord God, it is You who did sanctify the day by taking it for Yourself. Sanctify me in like manner by taking me for Yourself. Teach me so to enter into Your rest, so to find my rest in Your love, that my whole soul will be silent before You, in order that You may make Yourself and Your love known in

---

[8]Ps. 132:13,14

me. And let every Sabbath be to me a foretaste of the eternal rest with You. Amen.

Notes

1. The Sabbath was the first of all the ways of grace, instituted even before the Fall. You cannot set too high a value on it.

2. Observe how specially the Trinity has revealed Himself on the day of rest. The Father rested on this day. The Son rose from the dead on it. The Spirit sanctified this day by His special workings. You may expect the fellowship and the powerful workings of the Trinity on this day.

3. What is meant by the word "holy"? What is the day of rest a representation of according to Exodus 31, verse 13? How did God sanctify the day of rest? How does He sanctify us?

4. There are in this country certain difficulties in the way of the quiet celebration of the day of rest in a village where the church is often very full. Yet one can lay aside that which is unnecessary and receive the influx of company. We can fix an hour in which there will be reading and singing.

5. It is a matter of great importance to bring up children correctly for the sanctification of the Lord's day, by avoiding worldly society and conversation, by accustoming them to read something that may be useful for them. For the younger children, there should be a place in every Sunday school. It would be beneficial for the older children to come in contact with a book such as this, or a Bible, and have help to review the texts.

6. There is no better day than the Lord's day for giving food to body and soul. Let the work of Satan

on this day come to an end. Work for the heathen and the ignorant so that they may be carried forward.

7. The principal point is that the day of rest is the day of God's rest, of rest in and with God, and of fellowship with Him. It is God who will sanctify us. He does this by taking possession of us.

Chapter 42
Holy Baptism

"Go ye therefore, and teach all nations, baptizing them in the name of the Father and of the Son and of the Holy Ghost: teaching them to observe all things whatsoever I have commanded you" Matthew 28:19.

"He that believeth and is baptized shall be saved" Mark 16:16.

We find the meaning of the institution of baptism summarized in these words. The word "teach" means, "make disciples of all the nations, baptizing them." The believing disciple, as he is baptized in the water, is also to be baptized or introduced into the name of the Trinity.

By the name of the Father, the new birth and life as a child in the love of the Father are secured to him.[1] By the name of the Son, participation in the forgiveness of sins and the life that is in Christ are promised to him.[2] By the name of the Holy Spirit, the indwelling and progressive renewal of the Spirit are assured him.[3] And every baptized believer must always look upon baptism as his entrance into a covenant with the Trinity, and as a pledge that the Father, the Son, and the Spirit will, in course of time, do for him all that they have promised. It requires a lifelong study to know and enjoy all the

[1] Gal. 3:26,27; 4:67
[2] Col. 2:12
[3] Tit. 3:5,6

blessing that is presented in baptism.

In other passages of Scripture, the blessing is again set forth. We find bound up with it the new birth required to make a child of God. "Except a man be born of water and the Spirit, he cannot enter into the Kingdom of God" (John 3:5). The baptized disciple has in God a Father, and he has to live as a child in the love of this Father.[4]

Then, again, baptism is brought more directly into connection with the redemption that is in Christ. Consequently, the first and simplest representation of it is the forgiveness or washing away of sins. Forgiveness is always the gateway or entrance into all blessing. Therefore, baptism is also the sacrament of the beginning of the Christian life—a beginning that is maintained through the whole life. It is on this account that in Romans, chapter six, baptism is represented as the secret of the whole of sanctification, the entrance into a life in union with Jesus. "Know ye not that all we who were baptized into Christ Jesus were baptized into His death?" (Romans 6:3). The more precise explanation of what it is to be baptized into the death of Jesus, and to arise out of this with Him, for a new life in Him follows in verses 4-11. This is very powerfully comprehended elsewhere in this word, "As many of you as were baptized into Christ have put on Christ" (Galatians 3:27). This alone is the right life of a baptized disciple. He has put on Christ.[5] As one is plunged into water and passes under it, so is the believing confessor baptized into the death of Christ, in order then to live and walk clothed with

[4] John 3:3
[5] Rom. 6:3,4; Gal. 3:27; Col. 2:12

the new life of Christ.

And there are other passages where again the promise of the Spirit is connected with baptism. It is promised not only as the Spirit of regeneration but also as the gift from heaven bestowed on believers for indwelling and sealing—for progressive renewal. "He saved us through the washing of regeneration and renewing of the Holy Ghost, which He shed on us abundantly" (Titus 3:5,6). Here, renewal is the activity of the Spirit, by which the new life that is planted in the new birth penetrates our whole being, so that all our thinking and doing is sanctified by Him.[6]

And all this rich blessing which lies in baptism is received by faith. "He that believeth, and is baptized, shall be saved." Baptism was not only a confession on man's part of the faith that he already had, but equally a seal on God's part for the confirmation of faith—a covenant sign in which the whole treasury of grace lay open, to be enjoyed throughout life. As often as a baptized believer sees a baptism administered, or reflects on it, it is to be to him an encouragement to press, by an ever-growing faith, into the full life of salvation that the Trinity desires to work in him. The Holy Spirit is given to appropriate within us all the love of the Father and all the grace of the Son. The believing candidate for baptism is baptized into the death of Christ and has put on Christ. The Holy Spirit is in the disciple to give him all this as his daily experience.[7]

Lord God, make Your holy baptism always oper-

---

[6]Rom. 12:2; Eph. 4:23

[7]John 16:13,14; Eph. 4:14,15; Col. 2:6

ative in my soul as the experience that I am baptized into the death of Christ. And let Your people everywhere understand by Your Spirit what rich blessing lies in this baptism. Amen.

Chapter 43
The Lord's Supper

"The cup of blessing which we bless, is it not the communion of the blood of Christ? The bread which we break, is it not the communion of the body of Christ?" 1 Corinthians 10:16.

"He that eateth My flesh and drinketh My blood dwelleth in Me, and I in him. He that eateth Me, even shall he live by Me" John 6:56,57.

All life has need of food—it is sustained by nourishment which it takes in from without. The heavenly life must have heavenly food. Nothing less than Jesus Himself is the bread of life, "He that eateth Me even shall he live by Me."[1]

This heavenly food—Jesus—is brought near to us in two of the means of grace, the Word and the Lord's Supper. The Word comes to present Jesus to us from the side of the intellectual life, by our thoughts. The Lord's Supper comes in like manner to present Jesus to us from the side of the emotional life, by the physical senses. Man has a double nature—he has spirit and body. Redemption begins with the spirit, but it also penetrates to the body.[2] Redemption is not complete until this mortal body also shares in glory.

The Supper is the pledge that the Lord will also change our body of humiliation and make it like His

---

[1]Ps. 13:3; Matt. 4:4; John 6:51
[2]Rom. 8:23; 1 Cor. 6:13,15,19,20; Phil. 3:21

own glorified body by subduing all things to Himself. In the Supper, Christ would take possession of the whole man—body and soul—to renew and sanctify him by the power of His holy body and blood. Even His body shares in His glory. Even His body is communicated by the Holy Spirit. Even our body is fed with His holy body and renewed by the working of the Holy Spirit.[3]

This feeding with the body of Christ takes place, on the side of the Lord, by the Spirit; on our side, by faith.

This takes place on the side of the Lord by the Spirit. The Spirit communicates to us the power of the glorified body, by which our bodies become members of His body.[4] The Spirit also gives us to drink of the life-power of His blood, so that that blood becomes the life and the joy of our soul. The bread is a participation in the body. The cup is a participation in the blood.

And this takes place on our side by faith. A faith that, beyond what can be seen or understood, relies on the wonder-working power of the Holy Spirit to unite us with our Lord, in soul and body, by communicating Him inwardly to us.[5]

"What is it to eat the glorified body of Christ and to drink His shed blood?"

"It is not only to receive with a believing heart the whole suffering and dying of Christ, but also to be united more and more with His blessed body. It is to obtain forgiveness of sin and eternal life through the Holy Spirit who dwells in Christ and also in us. Even

---

[3]Matt. 26:26; John 6:54,55; Rom. 8:11,13
[4]1 Cor. 6:15,17; 12:13; Eph. 5:23,30
[5]Luke 1:37; 1 Cor. 2:9,12

though He is in heaven and we are on earth, it is to become flesh of His flesh and bone of His bone, and to live and be governed eternally by one Spirit."[6]

. This deeply inward union with Jesus, even with His body and blood, is the great aim of the Lord's Supper. All that it teaches and gives us of the forgiveness of sin, of the remembrance of Jesus, of the confirmation of the divine covenant, of union with one another, of the announcement of the Lord's death till He comes, must lead to this—complete oneness with Jesus through the Spirit.[7] "He that eateth My flesh and drinketh My blood dwelleth in Me, and I in him. He that eateth Me, even shall he live by Me."

It is readily understood that the blessing of the Supper depends very much on preparation within the inner chamber and on the hunger and thirst with which one longs for the living God.[8] Do not imagine, however, that the Supper is nothing but an outward symbol of what we already have by faith in the Word. No, it is an actual spiritual communication from the exalted Lord in heaven of the powers of His life. And it is this only according to the measure of desire and faith. Prepare for the Lord's Supper, therefore, with very earnest separation and prayer. And then surely expect that the Lord will, with His heavenly power, in a way incomprehensible to you, renew your life.

Blessed Lord, who instituted the Supper in order

---

[6]Catechism used by author in his church.

[7]Matt. 26:28; Luke 22:19; John 6:56; 15:4; I Cor. 10:17; 11:26; Rev. 3:20

[8]Job 11:13; Isa. 55:1,3; Matt. 5:6; Luke 1:53; I Cor. 11:28

to communicate Yourself to Your redeemed as their food and their power of life, teach us to use the Supper. Teach us at every opportunity to eat and to drink with great hunger and thirst for Yourself and for full union with You, believing that the Holy Spirit feeds us with Your body and gives us to drink of Your blood. Amen.

Notes

1. In connection with the Supper, let us be especially on our guard against the idea of a mere divine service of the congregation or transitory emotion. Preaching and addresses may make an edifying impression, while there is little power or blessing.

2. For a meal, the first requisite is hunger. A strong hunger and thirst for God is indispensable.

3. In the Supper, Jesus desires to give Himself to us and would have us give ourselves to Him. These are great and holy things.

4. The lessons of the Supper are many. It is a feast of remembrance; a feast of reconciliation; a feast of covenant; a feast of hope; a feast of love. But all these separate thoughts are only subordinate parts of the principal element—the living Jesus wants to give Himself to us in the most inward union. The Son of God wants to descend into our innermost parts. He wants to come to celebrate the Supper with us. "He that eateth My flesh and drinketh My blood, dwelleth in Me, and I in him."

5. And then union with Jesus is union with His people in love and sympathy.

6. The preparatory address is not itself the preparation. It is only a help to the private preparation which one must have in communion with Jesus.

7. To hold festival with God at His table is something of unspeakable importance. Please do not suppose that because you are a Christian it is easy for you to go and sit down. No, take time for solitude with Jesus so that He may speak to you and tell you how you should prepare your heart to eat with Him. It is very useful to take the whole week before the Supper for preparation and the whole week after for reflection.

Chapter 44
Obedience

"Now therefore, if ye will obey my voice indeed, ye shall be a peculiar treasure unto Me above all people" Exodus 19:5.

"The Lord shall greatly bless thee, if thou only carefully hearken unto the voice of the Lord thy God" Deuteronomy 15:4,5.

"By faith Abraham, when he was called, obeyed" Hebrews 11:8.

"Learned he obedience by the things which He suffered: and being made perfect, He became the author of eternal salvation unto all them that obey Him" Hebrews 5:8,9.

Obedience is one of the most important words in the Bible and in the life of the Christian. It was in the way of disobedience that man lost the favor and the life of God. It is only in the way of obedience that that favor and that life can again be enjoyed.[1] God cannot possibly take pleasure in, or bestow His blessing on, those who are not obedient. "If ye will obey My voice indeed, ye shall be a peculiar treasure unto Me"; "The Lord shall greatly bless thee, if thou only carefully hearken unto the voice of the Lord thy God." These alone are the eternal principles according to which man can enjoy God's favor and blessing.

We see this in the Lord Jesus. He says, "If ye keep

---

[1] Rom. 5:19; 6:16; 1 Pet. 1:2,14,22

My commandments, ye shall abide in My love; even
as I have kept my Father's commandments, and
abide in His love"(John 15:10). He was in the love of
the Father, but could not remain there except by
obedience. And He says that this is equally for us the
one way to continue in His love. We must keep His
commandments. He came to open for us the way
back to God. This way was the way of obedience.
Only he who, through faith in Jesus, walks in this
way will come to God.[2]

How gloriously this connection between the obedience of Jesus and our own is expressed in Hebrews
5, verses 8 and 9, "He learned obedience, and
became unto all them that obey Him the author of
eternal salvation." This is the bond of unity between
Jesus and His people, the point of conformity and
inward agreement. He was obedient to the Father
—they, on the other hand, are obedient to Him. He
and they are both obedient. His obedience not only
atones for, but drives out their disobedience. He and
they bear one mark—obedience to God.[3]

This obedience is a characteristic of the life of
faith. It is called the obedience of faith.[4] There is
nothing in earthly things that so spurs men to work
as faith. The belief that there is advantage or joy to
be found is the secret of all work. "By faith Abraham, when he was called, obeyed." My works will be
according to what I believe. The faith that Jesus
made me free from the power of sin for obedience,
and sets me in a suitable condition for it, has a
mighty power to make me obedient. Obedience is

[2]Gen. 22:17,18; 26:4,5; 1 Sam. 15:22
[3]Rom. 6:17; 2 Cor. 10:5; Phil. 2:8
[4]Acts 6:7; Rom. 1:5; 16:26

strengthened by faith: Faith in the overflowing blessing which the Father gives to obedience, in the promises of the love and indwelling of God, and in the promise of the fullness of the Spirit which comes by this channel.[5]

The power of this faith, again, as of obedience, lies especially in fellowship with the living God Himself. There is but one Hebrew word for "*obeying* voice" and "*hearing* voice." To hear correctly prepares one to obey. It is when I learn the will of God—not in the words of a man or a book—but from God Himself, and when I hear the *voic*e of God, that I will surely believe what is promised and do what is commanded. The Holy Spirit is the voice of God. When we hear the living voice speak, obedience becomes easy.[6] Let us wait in silence on God, and set our soul open before Him, so that He may speak by His Spirit. When, in our Bible reading and praying, we learn to wait more upon God so that we can say, "My God has spoken this to me, has given me this promise, has commanded this," then we will also obey. "To listen to the voice" earnestly, diligently, is the sure way to obedience.

With a servant, a warrior, a child, a subject, obedience is indispensable—the first sign of integrity. And will God, the living, glorious God, find no obedience with us?[7] No, let cheerful, punctual, precise obedience from the beginning be the mark of the genuineness of our fellowship with the Son whose obedience is our life.

---

[5]Deut. 28:1; Isa. 63:7-9; John 14:11,15,23; Acts 5:32
[6]Gen. 12:1,4; 31:13,16; Matt. 14:28; Luke 5:5; John 10:4,27
[7]Mal. 1:6; Matt. 7:21

Father, You make us Your children in Christ, make us in Him obedient children, as He was obedient. Let the Holy Spirit make the obedience of Jesus so glorious and powerful in us, that obedience will be the highest joy of our life. Teach us in everything only to seek to know what You desire and then to do it. Amen.

Notes

For a life of obedience, these things are required:

1. *Decisive surrender.* I must no longer have to ask in every single case, will I or will I not, must I, can I, be obedient? Now it must be such an unquestionable thing that I will know of nothing else than to be obedient. He who cherishes such a disposition, and thinks of obedience as a thing that stands firm, will find it easy, will literally taste great joy in it.

2. *The knowledge of God's will* through the Spirit. Please, do not imagine that because you know the Bible in some manner you know the will of God. The knowledge of God's will is something spiritual. Let the Holy Spirit make known to you the knowledge of God's will.

3. *The doing of all* that we know to be right. All doing teaches man. All doing of what is right teaches man obedience. All that the Word or conscience or the Spirit tells you is right, actually do it. It helps to form doing into a holy habit and is an exercise leading to more power and more knowledge. Do what is right, Christian, out of obedience to God, and you will be blessed.

4. *Faith in the power of Christ.* You have the power to obey. Be sure of this. Although you do not feel it, you have it in Christ your Lord by faith.

5. *The glad assurance of the blessing* of obedience. It unites us with our God; it wins His good pleasure and love; it strengthens our life; it brings the blessedness of heaven into our heart.

Chapter 45
The Will Of God

"Thy will be done, in earth as it is in heaven"
Matthew 6:10.

The glory of heaven, where the Father dwells, is that His will is done there. He who wants to taste the blessedness of heaven must know the Father who is there, and do His will, as it is done in heaven.[1]

Heaven is an unending holy Kingdom, of which the throne of God is the central point. Around this throne there are innumerable multitudes of pure, free beings, all ordered under powers and dominions. An indescribably rich and many-sided activity fills their life. All the highest and noblest that keeps man occupied is but a faint shadow of what takes place in this heavenly world. All these beings possess their free personal will. However, the will has, by its own choice, become one with the holy will of the Father, so that, in the midst of a diversity that flashes out in a million forms, only one will is accomplished—the will of God. All the rich, blessed movement of the inhabitants of heaven has its origin and its aim in the will of God.

And why is it then that His children on earth do not regard this will as their highest joy? Why is it that the petition, "Thy will be done in earth as it is in heaven," is often coupled with thoughts of the severe, trying elements in the will of God? Why is it coupled with thoughts of the impossibility of our

---

[1]Dan. 4:35

continually rejoicing in God's will? It is because we do not take pains to know the will of God in its glory and beauty. It is also because we do not know His will as the origin of love, as the source of power and joy, and as the expression of the perfection of God. We think of God's will only in the law that He gave and that we cannot keep, or in the trials in which His will appears in conflict with our own. Let us no longer do this, but take pains to understand that, in the will of God, all His love and blessedness can be comprehended and understood by us.[2]

Hear what the Word says about the will of God and the glorious things that are destined for us in this will.

"This is the will of my Father, that every one that seeth the Son and believeth on Him may have everlasting life" (John 6:40). The will of God is the rescue of sinners by faith in Christ. He who surrenders himself to this glorious will to seek souls will have the assurance that God will bless his work to others —for he carries out God's will, even as Jesus did it.[3]

"It is not the will of your Father which is in heaven that one of these little ones should perish" (Matthew 18:14). The will of God is the maintenance, the strengthening, and the keeping of the weakest of His children. What courage will he have who unites himself cordially with this will!

"This is the will of God, even your sanctification" (1 Thessalonians 4:3). With His whole heart, with all the power of His will, God is willing to make us holy. If we but open our heart and believe that it is not the law, but the will of God—something He certainly

---

[2]Gal. 1:4; Eph. 1:5,9,11; Heb. 10:10
[3]John 4:34; 5:20; 6:38,40

gives and does if we permit Him—then we will rejoice that our sanctification is stable and sure.[4]

"In everything give thanks: for this is the will of God in Christ Jesus concerning you" (1 Thessalonians 5:18). A joyful, thankful life is what God has destined for us and is what He will work in us. That which He desires, He certainly does for those who do not resist Him but receive and allow His will to work in them.

We must surrender our spirit to be filled with the thought—what God would have He will certainly bring to pass when we do not resist Him. And if we further consider how glorious and good and perfect the will of God is, then we will yield ourselves wholeheartedly so that this will may find its accomplishment in us.[5]

To this end, let us believe that the will of God is His love. Let us see what blessings in the Word are connected with the doing of this will.[6] Let us think of the glory of heaven as consisting of doing God's will, and make the choice that our life on earth will be in accordance with that will. And let us with prayer and meditation permit ourselves to be led by the Spirit to know this will completely.[7]

When we have learned to know the will of God on its glorious heavenly side in the Word—and have done it—it will not be difficult for us to also bear this will where it appears to be contrary to our nature. We will be so filled with the adoration of God and His will, that we will resolve to see and approve and

---

[4] 1 Thess. 5:23,24
[5] Rom. 12:2
[6] Matt. 7:21; 12:50; John 7:17; 9:31; Eph. 5:17; 6:6; 1 John 2:17
[7] Rom. 12:2; Col. 1:9; 4:12; Heb. 10:36; 13:21

love this will in everything. And it will be the most glorious thought of our life that there is to be nothing, *nothing*, in which the will of God must not be known and honored.[8]

Father, this was the glory of the Lord Jesus, that He did not do His own will, but the will of His Father. This glory I desire to have as mine. Father, open my eyes and my heart to know the perfection, the glory of Your will, and the glory of a life in this will. Teach me to understand Your will correctly, then willingly and cheerfully to execute it. When it becomes difficult for me, teach me to do Your will with loving adoration. Amen.

Notes

1. To do the will of God from the heart in prosperity is the only way to bear this will from the heart in suffering.

2. To do the will of God I must know it spiritually. The light and the power of the Spirit go together. What He teaches to see as God's will, He certainly teaches all to do. Meditate much on Romans 12:2, and pray earnestly to see God's will correctly.

3. Always learn to adore the will of God in the least and the worst thing that man does to you. It is not the will of God that man should do what is sinful. When man does sin, it is the will of God that His child should be thereby chastened. Say then always in the least as well as the greatest trials—it is the will of God that I am in this difficulty. This brings the soul to rest and silence, and teaches it to honor God in the trial.

---

[8]Matt. 26:39; Heb. 10:7,9

4. When God gave a will to man, He gave him a power whereby he could accept or reject the will of God with its full power. This is heavenly glory and blessedness, to be conscious that my will is in harmony with God's will. God's will lives in me. It is the will of God to work this in you.

Chapter 46
Self-Denial

"Then said Jesus unto His disciples, If any man will come after Me, let him deny himself, and take up his cross and follow Me" Matthew 16:24.

Self-denial was an exercise which the Lord Jesus often spoke about. Several times He mentioned it as an indispensable characteristic of every true disciple. He associates it with cross-bearing and losing our life.[1] Our old life is so sinful, and remains to the end so sinful, that it is never in a condition for anything good. Therefore, it must be denied and mortified so that the new life—the life of God—may have free reign in our lives.[2] From the very beginning, let the young Christian resolve to deny himself totally, in accordance with the command of his Lord. At the outset, it seems severe, but he will find that it is the source of inconceivable blessing.

Let self-denial reach our carnal understanding. It was when Peter had spoken according to the thought of the natural understanding that the Lord had to say to him, "Thou savourest not the things that be of God, but the things that be of men" (Matthew 16:23). You must deny yourselves and your own thoughts. In endeavoring to attain the knowledge of what God's will is, we must be careful that the activity of our understanding the Word and

---

[1]Matt. 10:38,39; Luke 9:23; 14:27; John 12:24,25
[2]Rom. 6:6; 8:13; Gal. 2:20; 5:24; 6:14; Col. 3:5

prayer does not deceive us with a service of God that is not in His Spirit and truth. Deny your carnal understanding. Bring it to silence, and in holy silence give place to the Holy Spirit. Let the voice of God be heard in your heart.[3]

Also, deny your own will, with all its lusts and desires. Once and for all, let it be unquestionable that the will of God is your choice in everything. Therefore, every desire that does not fall in with this will must be mortified. Please believe that in the will of God there is heavenly blessedness, and that therefore self-denial appears severe only at the outset. When you exercise yourself heartily in it, it becomes a great joy. Let the body with all its life remain under the law of self-denial.[4]

Also deny your own honor. Seek the honor of God. This brings such a rest into the soul. "How can ye believe," says Jesus, "which receive glory one of another?" (John 5:44). Although your honor may be hurt or reviled, commit it to God to watch over it. Be content to be little—to be nothing. "Blessed are the poor in spirit, for theirs is the Kingdom of heaven " (Matthew 5:3).[5]

Deny, in like manner, your own power. Cherish the deep conviction that it is those who are weak —those who are nothing—that God can use. Be very much afraid of your own endeavors in the service of God, however sincere they may be. Although you feel as if you had power, say before God that you do not have it—that your power is nothing. Continuous denial of your own power is the way to enjoy the

---

[3]Matt. 16:23; 1 Cor. 1:17,27; 2:6; Col. 2:18
[4]Matt. 26:39; Rom. 6:13; 1 Cor. 9:25,27
[5]John 7:18; 8:50; 1 Thess. 2:6

power of God. It is in the heart which dies to its own power that the Holy Spirit decides to live and bring the power of God.[6]

Especially deny your own interests. Do not live to please yourself, but your neighbor. He who seeks his own life will lose it. He who lives for himself will not find life. But he who truly imitates Jesus—to share in His joy—let him give his life as He did. Let him sacrifice his own interests.[7]

Beloved Christian, at conversion you had to make a choice between your own self and Christ. You said then, "Not I, but Christ" (Galatians 2:20). Now you are to confirm this choice every day. The more you do so, the more joyful and blessed it will be for you to renounce the sinful self—to cast aside unholy self-working—and allow Jesus to be all. The way of self-denial is a way of deep heavenly blessedness.

There are very many Christians who observe nothing of this way. They want Jesus to make them free from punishment, but not to liberate them from themselves—from their own will. But the invitation to discipleship always rings, "If any man will come after Me, let him deny himself, and take up his cross and follow Me."

We find the reason as well as the power for self-denial in the little word *Me*. "If any man will come after *Me*, let him deny *himself*, and follow *Me*." The old life is in ourselves. The new life is in Jesus. The new life cannot rule without driving out the old. Once one's own self had everything to say, now it must be nothing. But it would rather not be this.

---

[6] 2 Cor. 3:5; 12:9

[7] Rom. 15:1,3; 1 Cor. 10:23,24; Eph. 5:2

Because of this there must be denial of one's self and imitation of Jesus all day long. He, with His teaching, His will, and His honor, and His interests, must fill the heart. But he who has and knows Him willingly denies himself. Christ is so precious to him that he sacrifices everything, even himself, to win Him.[8]

This is the true life of faith. Not according to what nature sees or thinks to be acceptable, do I live, but according to what Jesus says and would have. Every day and every hour I confirm the wonderful thought, "Not I, but Christ" (Galatians 2:20). I am nothing, Christ is everything. "Ye are dead," and no longer have power, or will, or honor, "your life is hid with Christ in God" (Colossians 3:3). Christ's power and will alone prevail. Christians, cheerfully deny that sinful wretched self so that the glorious Christ may dwell in you.

Precious Savior, teach me what self-denial is. Teach me so to distrust my heart that in nothing will I yield to its fancy. Teach me to know You so that it will be impossible for me to do anything else than to offer up myself to possess You and Your life. Amen.

Notes

1. Of the denial of the natural understanding Tersteegen said, "God and His truth are never understood correctly except by the one who, by the dying of his carnal nature, his inclinations, passions, and will, is made very earnest and silent before God. This same soul must abandon the manifold deliberations of the understanding and become very simple and childlike. We must give our heart and our will

---

[8] Gal. 2:20; Phil. 3:7,8

entirely to God, forsaking our own will in all things, releasing ourselves especially from the manifold imaginations and activities of the understanding, even in spiritual things. Our understanding collects itself silently in the heart, and dwells as in the heart with God. Not in the head, but in the heart, does the true understanding display itself in acquiring the knowledge of God. In the head are the barren ideas of truth: in the heart is found the living truth itself, the anointing that teaches us all things. In the heart is found the living fountain of light. Anyone who lives in a heart entertained with God will often, with a glance of the eye, discern more truth than another with the greatest exertion."

2. Read the above passage with care. You will find in it the reason why we have said several times that when you read or pray you must at every opportunity keep quiet for a little while and set yourself in entire silence before God. This is necessary to bring the activity of the natural understanding to silence and to set the heart open before God so that He may speak there. The heart is the temple in which worship in spirit and truth takes place. Distrust and deny your understanding in spiritual things. The natural understanding is in the head. The spiritual understanding is in the heart, the temple of God. Preserve in the temple of God a holy silence before His countenance. Then He will speak.

3. The peculiar mark of Christian self-denial is inward cheerfulness and joy in the midst of turmoil. The Word of God makes unceasing joy a duty. This joyful disposition, hailing from eternity, has all change and variance under control and will hold its ground, not only in times of severe suffering, but

also in the self-denial of every day and hour that is inseparable from the Christian life.

4. What all am I to deny? Deny yourself. How will I know where and when to deny myself? Do so always and in everything. And if you do not understand that answer, know that no one can give you the right explanation of it but Jesus Himself. To imitate Jesus, to be taught of Him, is the only way to self-denial. Only when Jesus comes in does self go out.

Chapter 47

Discretion

"For wisdom entereth into thine heart, and knowledge is pleasant unto thy soul; discretion shall preserve thee, understanding shall keep thee" Proverbs 2:10,11.

"My son, keep sound wisdom and discretion: so shall they be life unto thy soul" Proverbs 3:21,22.

"Ye ought to be quiet, and to do nothing rash" Acts 19:36.

Indiscretion is not merely the sin of the unconverted. It often causes much evil and misery among the people of God. We read of Moses, "They angered him also at the waters of Meribah, so that it went ill with Moses for their sakes: because they were rebellious against his spirit, and he spake unadvisedly with his lips." So of Uzzah's touching the ark, "And God smote him there for his error" (2 Samuel 6:7).[1]

Discretion, and why it is so necessary, may be easily explained. When an army marches into the province of an enemy, its safety depends on the guards which are always on watch. The guards are to know and to give warning when the enemy approaches. Advance guards are sent out so that the territory and power of the enemy may be known. This prudence, which looks out beforehand and looks around, is dispensable.

---

[1]Ps. 106:33; Prov. 12:18

The Christian lives in the province of the enemy. All that surrounds him may become a snare or an occasion for sin. Therefore his whole walk is to be carried out in a holy reserve and watchfulness so that he may do nothing indiscreet. He watches and prays that he may not enter into temptation.[2] Prudence keeps guard over him.[3]

Discretion keeps watch over the lips. What loss many a child of God endures by thinking that if he speaks nothing wrong, he may speak what he will. He does not know how—through much speaking—the soul becomes ensnared in the distractions of the world. In the multitude of words there is not a lack of sin (Proverbs 10:19). Discretion endeavors not to speak unless it be for the glory of God and a blessing to neighbors.[4]

Discretion also keeps guard over the ear. All the news of the world comes to me through the gate of the ear—all the indiscreet speech of others—to infect me. Eagerness for news is very hurtful for the soul. Because of it, one can no longer look into one's self. One lives wholly in the world. Corinth was much more godless than Athens. But in the latter, where they "spent their time in nothing else but either to tell or to hear some new thing" (Acts 17:21), very few were converted. Take heed, says Jesus, what ye hear.[5]

On this account, discretion keeps watch over the society in which the Christian mingles. "Through desire a man, having separated himself, seeketh all

[2]Matt. 26:41; Luke 21:36; Eph. 6:18; 1 Pet. 4:7; 5:8

[3]1 Sam. 18:14; Matt. 10:16; Luke 1:17; 16:8; Eph. 5:15

[4]Ps. 39:2; 141:3; Prov. 10:19; Eccles. 5:1,2

[5]Prov. 2:2; 18:15; Mark 4:24

wisdom" (Proverbs 18:1). The child of God does not have the freedom to yield himself to the society of the world. He must know the will of his Father.[6]

Discretion keeps watch over all lawful occupations and possessions. It knows how gradually and secretly the love of money, worldly mindedness, and the secret power of the flesh, obtains the upper hand. It knows that it can never consider itself free from this temptation.[7]

And, above all, discretion keeps watch over the heart, because it is our life's fountain. Remembering the word, "he that trusteth in his own heart is a fool" (Proverbs 28:26), discretion walks in deep humility, and it works out salvation with fear and trembling.[8]

What source gives the soul the power to be endlessly on its guard against the thousand dangers surrounding it on all sides? Is it not fatiguing, exhausting, and harassing to have to thus watch always, and never to be at rest in the certainty that there is no danger? No, absolutely not. Discretion brings the highest restfulness. It has its security and strength in its heavenly Keeper, who does not slumber or sleep. In confidence in Him, under the inspiration of His Spirit, discretion does its work. The Christian walks wisely. The dignity of a holy prudence adorns him in all his actions. The rest of faith, the faith that Jesus watches and guards, binds us to Him in love. Holy discretion springs, as of its own accord, from a love that would not grieve or abandon Him, from a faith that has its strength for everything in Him.

---

[6]Ps. 1:1; 2 Cor. 6:14; 2 Thess. 3:14
[7]Matt. 13:22; Luke 21:34; 1 Tim. 6:9,17
[8]Prov. 3:21,23; 4:23; 28:18; Jer. 31:33

Lord my God, guard me so that I may not be indiscreet in heart. Let the prudence of the righteous always characterize me, in order that in everything I may be kept from giving offense. Amen.

Notes

1. It was once said to one who gave great care to having his horse and cart in thoroughly good order, "Come, it is not necessary to be taking so much trouble with this." His answer was, "I have always found that my prudence paid." How many a Christian has need of this lesson. How many a young Christian may well pray for this—that his conversion may be according to God's Word, "to the wisdom of the just" (Luke 1:17).

2. Discretion has its root in self-knowledge. The deeper my knowledge of my weakness and the sinfulness of my flesh is, the greater is the need for watchfulness. It is our element of true self-denial.

3. Discretion has its power in faith. The Lord is our Keeper and He does His keeping through the Spirit. It is from Him that our discretion comes.

4. Its activity is not limited to ourselves. Discretion reaches out to our neighbor, in the way of giving him no offense, and in laying no stumbling block in his way (Rom. 14:13; 1 Cor. 8:9; 10:32; Phil. 1:10).

5. Discretion finds great delight in silence so as to commit its way to the Lord with composure and deliberation. It esteems highly the word of the town-clerk of Ephesus, "Ye ought to be quiet, and to do nothing rash" (Acts 19:36).

6. In great generals and their victories we see that discretion is not timidity. It is consistent with the

highest courage and the most joyful certainty of victory. Discretion watches against rashness but enhances the courage of faith.

Chapter 48
Money

"Money answereth all things" Ecclesiastes 10:19.

"I had wholly dedicated the silver unto the Lord from my hand" Judges 17:3.

"Thou oughtest therefore to have put my money to the exchangers, and then at my coming I should have received mine own with usury" Matthew 25:27.

In his dealing with the world and its possessions, the Christian finds an opportunity to manifest his self-denial and the spirit of discretion.[1] Since all value or property on earth still finds its expression in money, it is in his dealings with money that he can especially show he is free from worldliness by denying himself to serve his God. In order to thoroughly comprehend this, we must consider what is to be said about money.

What does money represent? It represents the work by which a man earns it and his industry, zeal, and ability in that work. It is indicative of his success and the blessing of God upon the work. It also represents all that I can do with money and the work that others would do for me. It signifies the power that I have to accomplish what I desire and the influence which I exercise on those who are dependent on me for my money. It is a representation of all the possessions or enjoyments that are to be obtained by money and of all on earth that can make life desirable. Yes, it represents life itself, without

[1]John 17:15,16; 1 Cor. 7:31

which the purchase of indispensable food cannot be supported.

Money is, indeed, one of the most desirable and fruitful of earthly things. No wonder that it is so esteemed by all.

What is the danger of money? What sin does it lead to, that the Bible and experience should so warn us to be prudent in dealing with it? There is the anxiousness that occurs when one does not know if there will be sufficient money.[2] There is the covetousness that longs too much for it.[3] There is the dishonesty that, without gross deception or theft, does not give to a neighbor what belongs to him.[4] There is the lovelessness that desires to draw everything to one's self and does not help another.[5] There is the love of money, which greedily seeks after riches and lands.[6] There is the robbery of God and the poor in withholding the share that belongs to them.[7]

What is the blessing of money? If the danger of sin is so great, would it not be better if there were no money? Is it not better to be without money? No, even for the spiritual life money may be a great blessing. It may be an exercise in industry and activity,[8] in care and economy. It may be a sign of God's blessing upon our work.[9] It may be an opportunity

---

[2]Matt. 6:31
[3]1 John 2:15,16
[4]Jas. 5:4
[5]Luke 16:19,25
[6]1 Tim. 6:9,10,17
[7]Prov. 3:27,28; Mal. 3:8
[8]Eccles. 5:18,19
[9]Prov. 10:4.22

for showing that we can possess and lay it out for God, without withholding it or cleaving to it, and that by means of it we can manifest our generosity to the poor and our overflowing love for God's cause.[10] It may be a means of glorifying God by our charity and of spreading among men the gold of heavenly blessing.[11] It may be a thing that, according to the assurance of Jesus, we can exchange for a treasure in heaven.[12]

And what is now the way to be freed from the danger and to be led into the righteous blessing of money?

Let God be Lord over your money. Receive all your money with thanksgiving, as coming from God in answer to the prayer, "Give us this day our daily bread"(Matthew 6:11).[13]

Lay it all down before God as belonging to Him. Say with the woman, "I had wholly dedicated the silver unto the Lord" (Judges 17:3).[14]

Let your dealing with your money be a part of your spiritual life. Receive and possess and give out your money as one who has been bought at a high price—redeemed, not with silver and gold, but with the precious blood of Jesus.[15]

Make what the Word of God says of money—of earthly goods—a special study. The Word of the Father alone teaches how the child of God is to use blessing.

---

[10] 2 Cor. 8:14,15
[11] 2 Cor. 9:12,13
[12] Matt. 19:21; Luke 12:33
[13] 1 Chron. 29:14
[14] 1 Chron. 29:12,14
[15] Luke 19:8; 1 Pet. 1:18,19

Greatly reflect on the fact that it is not given to you for yourself alone, but for you and your brethren together. The blessing of money is to do good to others and to make them rejoice.[16]

Remember that it can be given up to the Father and the service of His Kingdom for the upbuilding of His spiritual temple—the extension of His influence. Every time a spiritual blessing is mentioned in Scripture, it is a time of cheerful giving for God's cause. Even the outpouring of the Holy Spirit made itself known in the giving of money for the Lord.[17]

Christian, understand this, all the deepest deliberations of the heart and its most spiritual activities can manifest themselves in the way in which we deal with our money. Love to God, love to our neighbor, victory over the world by faith, the hope of everlasting treasure, faithfulness as a steward, joy in God's service, cheerful self-denial, holy discretion, and the glorious freedom of the children of God, can all be seen in the use of money. Money can be the means of the most glorious fellowship with God and the full enjoyment of the blessedness of being able to honor and serve Him.

Lord God, make me properly discern in what close connection my money stands with my spiritual life. Let the Holy Spirit lead and sanctify me, so that all my earning and receiving, my keeping and dispensing of money, may always be pleasing to You and a blessing to my soul. Amen.

---

[16]Acts 20:35
[17]Ex. 36:5; 1 Chron. 29:6,9; Acts 2:45; 4:34

Notes

1. John Wesley always said that there were three rules about the use of money which he gave to men in business and by which he was sure that they would experience benefit.

—Make as much money as you can. Be industrious and diligent.

—Save as much money as you can. Be no spendthrift, live frugally and prudently.

—Give away as much money as you can. That is the divine destination of money. That makes it an everlasting blessing for yourselves and others.

2. Acquaint yourself with the magnificent prayer of David in 1 Chronicles 29:10-20. Receive it into your soul because it teaches us the blessedness and the glorification of God that springs from cheerful giving.

Chapter 49
The Freedom Of The Christian

"Being then made free from sin, ye became the servants of righteousness. Being made free from sin, ye have your fruit unto holiness" Romans 6:18,22.

"But now we are delivered from the law" Romans 7:6.

"The law of the Spirit of life in Christ Jesus hath made me free from the law of sin and death" Romans 8:2.

Freedom is counted in Scripture as one of the greatest privileges of the child of God. Throughout history, there is nothing for which nations have made great sacrifices except freedom. Slavery is the lowest condition into which man can sink, for in it he can no longer govern himself. Freedom is the deepest need of his nature.

To be free, then, is the condition in which anything can develop itself according to the law of its nature—according to its own disposition. Without freedom nothing can attain its destiny or become what it should be. This is true of the animal and man, of the worldly and the spiritual alike. It was for this reason that God chose the redemption of Israel out of the slavery of Egypt and into the glorious liberty of the promised land as the everlasting example of redemption out of the slavery of sin and into the liberty of the children of God.[1] On this account,

---

[1]Ex. 1:14; 4:23; 6:5; 20:2; Deut. 24:18

Jesus said, "If the Son therefore shall make you free, ye shall be free indeed" (John 8:36). And the Holy Scriptures teach us to stand firmly in the freedom with which Christ made us free. Complete insight into this freedom opens up to us one of the greatest glories of the life that the grace of God has prepared for us.[2]

There are three passages from the Epistle to the Romans which speak of our sanctification through a threefold freedom. There is freedom from sin in the sixth chapter, freedom from the law in the seventh, and freedom from the law of sin in the eighth.

There is freedom from sin (Romans 6:7,18,22). Sin is represented as a power that rules over man, and under which he is brought and taken captive. It urges him to be a slave to evil.[3] By the death *of* Christ and *in* Christ, the believer—who is one with Him—is made entirely free from the dominion of sin. It has no more power over him. If, then, he still sins, it is because he permits sin still to rule over him, not knowing his freedom by faith. But if by faith he fully accepts what the Word of God thus confirms, then sin has no power over him. He overcomes it by the faith that he is made free from it.[4]

Then there is freedom from the law. This leads us deeper into the life of grace than freedom from sin. According to Scripture, law and sin always go together. "The strength of sin is the law" (1 Corinthians 15:56). The law does nothing but make the offense greater.[5] The law reveals our sinfulness. It

[2]John 8:32; Gal. 4:21,31; 5:1

[3]John 8:34; Rom. 7:14,23; 2 Pet. 2:19

[4]Rom. 5:21; 6:13,14

[5]Rom. 4:15; 5:13,20; 7:13

cannot help us against sin; rather, with its demand for perfect obedience, it hopelessly gives us over to the power of sin. The Christian who does not realize that he is made free from the law will still always abide under sin.[6] Christ and the law cannot rule over us together. In every endeavor to fulfill the law as believers, we are taken captive by sin.[7] The Christian must know that he is entirely free from the law—from the *you must* that stands around us and over us. Then, for the first time, he will know what it is to be free from sin.

Then there is also freedom from the law of sin—actual liberation from the power of sin in our members. What we have in Christ, freedom from sin and from the law, is inwardly appropriated for us by the Spirit of God. "The law of the Spirit of life in Christ Jesus hath made me free from the law of sin and death." The Holy Spirit in us takes the place of the law over us. "If ye be led of the Spirit, ye are not under the law" (Galatians 5:18). Freedom from the law is not anything external. Instead, it takes place according to the amount of dominion and leading of the Spirit within us. "Where the Spirit of the Lord is, there is liberty" (2 Corinthians 3:17). Accordingly, as the law of the Spirit rules in us, we are made free from the law, and from the law of sin. We are then free to do what we, as God's children, would gladly do—serve God.

Free expresses a condition in which nothing hinders me from being what I could and should be. In other words, *free* is to be able to do what I desire. The power of sin over us, the power of the law

---

[6]Rom. 6:15; 7:5
[7]Rom. 7:5,23

against us, and the power of the law of sin in us, hinder us. But he who stands in the freedom of the Holy Spirit—he who is then truly free—cannot be prevented or hindered from being what he could and should be. As it is the nature of a tree to grow upwards—free from all hindrances—so a child of God then grows to what he should and will be. As the Holy Spirit leads him into this freedom, the joyful consciousness of his strength for the life of faith springs up. He shouts joyfully, "I can do all things through Him which strengtheneth me" (Philippians 4:13). "Thanks be unto God which always causeth us to triumph in Christ" (2 Corinthians 2:14).

Son of God, anointed with the Spirit to announce freedom to the captives, make me also truly free. Let the Spirit of life in You, my Lord, make me free from the law of sin and of death. I am Your ransomed one. Let me live as Your freed one, who is hindered by nothing from serving You. Amen.

Notes

1. The freedom of the Christian extends over his whole life. He is free in relation to the institutions and teachings of men. "Ye are bought with a price: be ye not the servants of men" (1 Cor. 7:23; Col. 2:20). He is free in relation to the world and in the use of what God gives. He has power to possess it or to dispense with it, to enjoy it or to sacrifice it (1 Cor. 9:1).

2. This freedom is no lawlessness. We are free from sin and the law to serve God in the Spirit. We are not under the law, but give ourselves, with free

choice and in love, to Him who loves us (Rom. 6:18; Gal. 5:13; 1 Pet. 2:16). Not under the law, also not without the law, but in the law—a new and higher law. "The law of the Spirit of life," "the law of liberty," (1 Cor. 9:21; Jas. 1:15; 2:12), the law written in our hearts, is our rule and measure. In this last passage the translation ought to be, "bound by a law to Christ."

3. This freedom has its subsistence from and in the Word. The more the Word abides in me and the truth lives in me, the freer I become (John 8:31,32,36).

4. Freedom manifests itself in love. I am free from the law and from man and from institutions to be able now, like Christ, to surrender myself for others (Rom. 14:13,21; Gal. 5:13; 6:1).

5. This glorious liberty to serve God and our neighbor in love is a spiritual thing. We cannot by any means seize it and draw it to us. It becomes known only by a life in the Holy Spirit. "Where the Spirit of the Lord is, there is liberty" (2 Cor. 3:17). "If ye be led of the Spirit, ye are not under the law" (Gal. 5:18). It is the Holy Spirit who makes us free. Let us allow ourselves to be introduced by Him into the effectual, glorious liberty of the children of God. "The Spirit of life in Christ Jesus hath made me free from the law of sin and death" (Rom. 8:2).

Chapter 50
Growth

"So is the kingdom of God, as if a man should cast seed into the ground; and should sleep and rise night and day, and the seed should spring forth and grow up, he knoweth not how. The earth bringeth forth fruit of herself; first the blade, after that the ear, then the full corn in the ear" Mark 4:26-28.

"The Head, from which all the body increaseth with the increase of God" Colossians 2:19.

"That we may grow into Him in all things, which is the Head, even Christ, from whom the whole body maketh the increase" Ephesians 4:15,16.

Life is continual movement, progressiveness. Increase or growth is the law of all created life. Consequently, the new life in man is destined to increase—always by becoming stronger. As there are in the seed and in the earth a life and power of growth which impels the plant to achieve its full height and fruit, so is there in the seed of the eternal life an impelling force by which that life always increases and grows. This divine growth continues until we come to be a perfect man—measuring up to the stature of the fullness of Christ.[1]

In this parable of the seed that springs up of itself, and becomes great and bears fruit, the Lord teaches us two of the most important lessons on the increase of the spiritual life. The one is that of its *self-*

---
[1]Eph. 4:13; 2 Thess. 1:3,4

241

sufficiency; the other is that of its *gradual timing*.

The first lesson is for those who ask what they are to do in order to grow and advance more in grace. As the Lord said of the body, "Which of you by being anxious can add one cubit unto his stature? Consider the lilies of the field how they grow" (Matthew 6:27,28). So He says to us here that we can do nothing, and need to do nothing, to make the spiritual life grow.[2] Do you not see how, while man slept, the seed sprang up and became high? Do you not see that he did not know how the earth brought forth fruit by itself? Once man has sown, he must believe that God cares for the growth. Man does not have to care. He must trust and rest.

And must man then do nothing? You must understand that he can do nothing. The power of life must come from within—from the life and the Spirit implanted in him. He can contribute nothing to the growth itself. His growth will be given to him.[3]

All he can do is to let the life grow. All that can hinder the life, he must take away and keep away. He can take away any thorns and thistles in the soil which occupy the place and power that the plant should have.[4] The plant must have its place in the earth alone and undivided. The farmer can care for this. Then it is able to grow further *of itself*. Likewise, the Christian must take away what can hinder the growth of the new life. He must surrender his heart entirely and completely for the new life, allowing it alone to possess his heart, so that it may grow

---

[2] Hos. 14:5; Matt. 6:25,30

[3] Ps. 92:12,13; Gal. 2:20; Col. 3:3

[4] Matt. 13:22,23; John 15:1,2

free and unhindered.[5]

The farmer can also bring forth what the plant requires in the way of food or drink. He can manure or moisten the soil as it is needed. So must the believer see to it that for the new life nourishment is brought forth out of the Word, the living water of the Spirit, by prayer. It is in Christ that the new life is planted. From Him it increases with divine increase. Stay rooted in Him by the exercise of faith, and the life will grow of itself.[6] Give it what it must have, take away what can hinder it, and the life will grow and increase of itself.

Then comes the second lesson of the parable—the gradual timing of the growth, "first the blade, after that the ear, then the full corn in the ear." Do not expect everything at once. Give God time. By faith and endurance we inherit the promises—faith that knows that it has everything in Christ, and endurance that expects everything in its time according to the rule and the order of the divine government. Give God time. Give the new life time. It is by continually remaining in the earth that the plant grows. It is by continually standing in grace, in Christ Himself—in whom God has planted us—that the new life grows.[7]

Yes, give the new life sufficient time—time in prayer, time in communion with God, time in continuous exercise of faith, and time in persistent separation from the world. Give it time. The divine inner growth with which the life of God perfects man in Christ is slow but sure, hidden but real, and weak

---

[5]Song 2:15; Heb. 12:1
[6]John 15:4,5; Col. 2:6,7
[7]Heb. 3:13; 6:12,15; Jas. 5:7

but endowed with heavenly power.

Lord God, graciously strengthen the faith of Your children, showing them that their growth and progress are in Your hands. Enable them to see what a precious, powerful life was implanted in them by You—a life that increases with a divine increase. Enable them, by faith and patience, to inherit the promises. And teach them in that faith to take away all that can hinder the new life, and to bring forward all that can further it, so that You may make Your work in them glorious. Amen.

Notes

1. For the plant, the principal thing is the soil in which it stands and out of which it draws its strength. For the Christian, this also is the principal thing. He is in Christ. Christ is all. He must grow up in Him, for out of Him the body obtains its increase. The main thing is to abide in Christ by faith.

2. Remember that faith must set itself toward a silent restfulness so that growth is just like that of the lilies of God's hands, and so that He will see to it that we increase and grow strong.

3. By this firm and joyful faith we become "Strengthened with all might according to His glorious power, unto all patience and longsuffering with joyfulness" (Col. 1:11).

4. This faith that God cares for our growth takes away all anxiety and gives courage for doing the two things that we have to do—the taking away of what might be obstructive to the new life, and the bringing forward of what may be serviceable to it.

5. Observe well the distinction between planting

and growing. Planting is the work of a moment. In a moment the earth receives the seed. After that comes the slow growth. Without delay—immediately—the sinner must receive the Word. There can be no delay before conversion. Then, with time, the growth of the seed follows.

6. The main thing is Christ. From Him and in Him is our growth. He is the soil that of itself brings forth fruit, yet we do not know how. Hold fellowship with Him daily. A month's worth of meditations on the blessed life of continued fellowship with Him are provided in my book, *Abide in Christ*.

Chapter 51
Searching The Scriptures

"O how I love Thy law! it is my meditation all the day" Psalm 119:97.

"Search the Scriptures: and they are they which testify of Me" John 5:39.

"The word preached did not profit them, not being mixed with faith in them that heard" Hebrews 4:2.

At the beginning of this book there is more than one passage on the use of God's Word in the life of grace. Before I take leave of my readers, I would like to come back to this all-important point. I cannot too earnestly and urgently address this call to my young brothers and sisters—your spiritual life greatly depends on your use of God's Word.

Man lives by the Word that comes from the mouth of God. Therefore, seek with your whole heart to learn how to use God's Word correctly. With this in mind, reflect on the following hints:

Read the Word *more with the heart than with the understanding*. With the understanding I know and comprehend—with the heart I desire and love and hold firmly. Let the understanding be the servant of the heart. Be very afraid of your understanding or carnal nature, which cannot receive spiritual things.[1] Deny your understanding, and wait in humility on the Spirit of God. On every occasion, keep silent

---

[1] 1 Cor. 1:21,27; 2:6,12,14; Col. 2:18,23

during your reading of the Word. Say to yourselves, "This Word I now receive in my heart, to love and to let it live in me."[2]

Always read the Word *in fellowship with the living God*. The power of a word depends on my conviction regarding the man who wrote it. First, set yourself in loving fellowship with the living God under the impression of His nearness and love. Deal with the Word under the full conviction that He, the eternal God, is speaking with you. Let your heart be silent while you listen to God—to God Himself.[3] Then the Word will certainly become a great blessing to you.

Read the Word *as a living Word in which the Spirit of God dwells, and that certainly works in those who believe*. The Word is seed. Seed has life, and grows and yields fruit of itself. Likewise, the Word has life, and of itself grows and yields fruit.[4] If you do not wholly understand it—if you do not feel its power—carry it in your heart. Ponder it and meditate on it, and it will of itself begin to yield a working and growth in you.[5] The Spirit of God is with and in the Word.

Read it *with the resolve to be, not only a hearer, but a doer of the Word*. Let the great question be—What would God now have of me with this Word? If the answer is—He would have me believe it and rely on Him to fulfill it—immediately do this from the heart. If the Word is a command of what

---

[2]Ps. 119:10,11,47; Rom. 10:18; Jas. 1:21

[3]Gen. 17:3; 1 Sam. 3:9,10; Isa. 50:4; 52:6; Jer. 1:2

[4]Mark 4:26,27,28; John 6:63; 1 Thess. 2:13; 1 Pet. 1:23

[5]Ps. 119:15,40,48,69; 2 Tim. 3:16,17

you are to do, immediately yield yourself to do it.[6] There is an unspeakable blessedness in the doing of God's Word, and in the surrender of myself to be and to act just as His Word dictates. Do not be only hearers, but doers of the Word.

Read the Word *with time*. More and more, I see that one obtains nothing on earth without time. Give the Word time. Give the Word time to come into your heart, on every occasion on which you sit down to read it. Give it time, in the persistence with which you are faithful to it, from day to day and month to month.[7] With perseverance, you become exercised and more accustomed to the Word and the Word begins to work. Please, do not be discouraged when you do not understand the Word. Hold on, take courage, give the Word time. Later on the Word will explain itself. David had to meditate day and night to understand it.

Read the Word *with a searching of the Scriptures*. The best explanation of the Bible is the Bible itself. Take three or four texts on one point, and set them close to one another and compare them. See where they agree and where they differ. See where they say the same thing or again something else. Let the Word of God in one place be cleared up and confirmed by what He said in another place on the same subject. This is the safest and the best explanation. Even the holy writers used this method of instruction with the Scriptures, *"and again"* (John 19:37).[8] Do not complain that this method takes too much

---

[6]Matt. 5:19,20; 7:21,24; Luke 11:28; Jas. 1:21,25

[7]Deut. 6:5-9; Ps. 1:2; 119:97; Jer. 15:16

[8]Isa. 34:16; John 5:39; Acts 17:11; Heb. 2:13

time and energy. It is worth the trouble. Your pains will be rewarded. On earth you have nothing without effort.[9] He who wants to go to heaven never goes without taking pains. Search the Scriptures, you will be richly rewarded.

Young Christian, let one of my last and most earnest words to you be this—your growth, your power, and your life depend on your faithfulness to the Word of God. Love God's Word. Esteem it sweeter than honey, better than thousands in silver or gold. In the Word, the Father can and will reveal His heart to you. In the Word, Jesus will communicate Himself and all His grace. In the Word, the Holy Spirit will come into you, to renew your heart and all your thoughts, according to the mind and will of God. Do not simply read enough of the Word to keep you from falling away. Make it one of your chief occupations on earth, to yield yourself so that God may fill you with His Word, and may fulfill His Word in you.

Lord God, what grace it is that You speak to us in Your Word, that we in Your Word have access to Your heart, to Your will, and to Your love. Forgive us for our sins against Your precious Word. And, Lord, let the new life become so strong by the Spirit in us, that all its desire will be to abide in Your Word. Amen.

Notes

1. In the middle of the Bible stands Psalm 119, in which the praise and the love of God's Word are so strikingly expressed. It is not enough for us to read

---

[9] Prov. 2:4,5; 3:13,18; Matt. 13:44

through the divisions of this psalm successively. We must take its principal points and seek what is said in different passages upon each of these points. Let us, for example, take the following points, observing the indications of the answers, and seek in this way to come under the full impression of what is taught us of the glory of God's Word:

a. The blessing that the Word gives—verses 1,2,6,9,11,24,45,46,47,etc.

b. How we have to handle the Word (observe, walk, keep, mark, etc.).

c. The names that are given to God's Word in this psalm.

d. Prayer for divine teaching—verses 5,10,12, 18,19,26.

e. Surrender to obedience to the Word— verses 93,105,106,112,128,133.

f. God's Word, the basis of prayer—verses 41,49,58,76,107,116,170.

g. Observance as the ground of confidence in prayer—verses 77,159,176.

h. Observance as promised upon the hearing of prayer—verses 8,17,33,34,44.

i. The power to observe the Word—verses 32,36,41,42,117,135,146.

j. The praise of God's Word—verses 54,72,97,129,130,144.

k. The confident confession of obedience— verses 102,110,121,168.

l. Personal fellowship with God, seen in the psalmist's use of Thou and I, Thine and Mine.

I have merely mentioned a few points and a few verses. Seek out more and mark them until your mind is filled with the thoughts about the Word which the Spirit of God desires to give you. Read the words of that great man of faith, George Muller, with great thoughtfulness. He says, "The power of our spiritual life will be according to the measure of the room that the Word of God takes up in our life and in our thoughts. After an experience of fifty-four years, I can solemnly declare this. For three years after my conversion I used the Word little. Since that time, I have searched it with diligence, and the blessing was wonderful. From that time, I have read the Bible through a hundred times and at every time with increasing joy. Whenever I start afresh with it, it appears to me as a new book. I cannot express how great the blessing is of faithful, daily, regular searching of the Bible. The day is lost for me on which I have used no solid time for enjoying the Word of God.

"Friends sometimes say: 'I have so much to do that I can find no time for regular Bible study.' I believe that there are few that have to work harder than I have. Yet it remains a rule with me never to begin my work until I have had real, sweet fellowship with God. After that I give myself heartily to the business of the day, that is, to God's work, with only intervals of some minutes for prayer."

Chapter 52

The Lord The Perfecter

"I will cry unto God most High; unto God that performeth all things for me" Psalm 57:2.

"The Lord will perfect that which concerneth me" Psalm 138:8.

"Being confident of this very thing, that He which hath begun a good work in you will perform it until the day of Jesus Christ" Philippians 1:6.

"For of Him, and through Him, and to Him are all things: To whom be glory for ever" Romans 11:36.

We read that David once succumbed to unbelief, and said, "I shall now one day perish by the hand of Saul" (1 Samuel 27:1). So even the Christian may indeed fear that he will one day perish. This is because he looks at himself and what is in him, and does not set his trust wholly on God. It is because he does not yet know God as the Perfecter. He does not yet know what is meant by His name, "I am the Alpha and the Omega: the Beginning and the End: the First and the Last" (Revelation 21:6; 1:8). If I truly believe in God as the beginning out of whom all comes, then I must trust Him as the continuation and the end, to whom all goes.

God is the beginning. "He which hath begun a good work in you"; "Ye have not chosen Me, but I have chosen you" (John 15:16). We are to be thankful for God's free choice, made before the foundation of the world, that we became believers and have the new life.[1] Those who are still unconverted have nothing to do with this election—for them there is the offer of grace and the summons to surrender.

Outside, over the door of the Father, stands the inscription, "Him that cometh unto Me, I will in no wise cast out" (John 6:37). This everyone can see and understand. No sooner are they inside the door than they see and understand the other inscription, "All that the Father giveth Me shall come to Me" (John 6:37).[2] Then they can understand how all things are of God—first, obedience to the command of God, then, insight into the counsel of God.

But then it is of great importance to firmly hold onto this truth—He has begun the good work. Every thought of God will strengthen the confidence that He will also perfect it. His faithfulness, His love, His power, are all pledged so that He will perfect the good work which He began. Please read how God has taken more than one oath regarding His unchangeable faithfulness. Your soul will rest and find courage in this.

And how will He finish His work? What has its origin *from* Him is sustained *by* Him. It will one day be brought *to* Him and His glory. There is nothing in your life, worldly or spiritual, for which the Father will not care, because it has influence on you for eternity.[3] There is no moment of day or night in which the silent growth of your soul is not to go forward. The Father will take care of this, if you believe.

There is no part of your destiny as a child of God

---

[1] Rom. 8:29,30; Eph. 1:4,11
[2] Gen. 28:15; Ps. 89:29,34-36; Isa. 54:9,10; Jer. 33:25,26
[3] Matt. 6:25,34; 1 Pet. 5:7

that the Father will not continue and complete His work in—even in things which you have not yet given thought to.[4] There is one condition—you must trust Him for this. You must in faith allow Him to work. You must trustfully say, "The Lord will perfect that which concerneth me." You must trustfully pray, "I will cry unto God that performeth all things for me." Christian, let your soul become full of the thought—The whole care, for the continuation and the perfecting of God's work in me, is in His hands.[5]

And how glorious the perfecting will be. In our spiritual life, God is prepared to exhibit His power in making us participants of His holiness and the image of His Son. He will make us fit, and set us in a condition for all the blessed work in His Kingdom that He would have from us. He will make our body like to the glorious body of His Son. We may wait for the coming of the Son Himself from heaven to take His own to Him. He will unite us in one body with all His chosen, and will receive and make us dwell forever in His glory. How can we think that God will not perfect His work? He will surely do it—He will gloriously do it—for everyone who trusts Him for it.

Child of God, please say in deep assurance of faith, "The Lord will perfect that which concerneth me." In every need say continually and with great boldness, "I will call on God, that performeth all things for me." And let the song of your life be the joyful doxology, "For of Him, and through Him, and to Him are all things: To Him be the glory for ever." Amen.

---

[4] Isa. 27:2,3; 51:12,13
[5] Heb. 10:35; 13:5,6,20,21; 1 Pet. 5:10

Lord God, who will perfect that which concerns me, teach me to know You and to trust You. And let every thought of the new life go hand in hand with the joyful assurance—He who began a good work in me will perfect it. Amen.

Notes

1. "He that endureth to the end, shall be saved" (Matt. 10:22). It brings but little profit to begin well. We must hold the beginning of our hope firm unto the end (Matt. 10:27; 24:13; Heb. 3:14,16; 11:12).

2. How do we explain the falling away of some believers? They were only temporary believers. They were partakers only of the workings of the Spirit (Heb. 6:4).

3. How do I know whether I am a partaker of the true new birth? "As many as are led by the Spirit of God, they are the sons of God" (Rom. 8:14). The faith that God has received me is matured—is confirmed—by works and by a walk under the leading of the Spirit.

4. How can any one know for certain that he will persevere to the end? By faith in God the Perfecter. We may take the Almighty God as our Keeper. He who gives himself in sincerity to Him, and trusts wholly in Him to perfect His work, obtains a divine certainty that the Lord has him and will hold him firm unto the end.

5. Child of God, live in fellowship with your Father. Live the life of faith in your Jesus with an undivided heart, and all fear of falling away will be taken from you. The living seal of the Holy Spirit will be your assurance of perseverance to the end.